Praise for

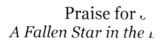

A Fallen Star in the ... the Kid

". . .The picture of Juan Patrón that emerges here is largely that of a genuine, intelligent, honest, industrious man, but undoubtedly one with a dark strain in his personality. Even so, it is not too difficult to imagine that had he been born a decade or two later in a settled and more tolerant society, he might well have become New Mexico's first Congressman when statehood was conferred in 1912. This recognition of his achievements and premature death is long overdue, and I commend both it and its author to you."

—Frederick Nolan, Chalfont St Giles, England, author of *The West of Billy the Kid* and *The Lincoln County War: A Documentary History*

"A biography of Juan B. Patrón has long been awaited by students of New Mexico's inglorious Lincoln County War. Paul L. Tsompanas provides us a readable account of his rise from a minor county official to Speaker of the House in Santa Fe and to his violent death at age 32.

Now best remembered for his brief association with Billy the Kid, Patrón stands today as one of the most visible Hispanic figures whose career interacted with the War. Tsompanas' well-researched study of his life will be welcomed by readers endlessly fascinated by Lincoln County's troubles."

–Marc Simmons, historian

JUAN PATRÓN

JUAN PATRÓN

A Fallen Star in the Days of Billy the Kid

PAUL L. TSOMPANAS

BELLE ISLE BOOKS
www.belleislebooks.com

Front cover image credit: The portrait of Juan Patrón was done by Bob Boze Bell, an artist, humorist and editor of *True West* Magazine. The original work is owned by Cleis and Jerome Jordon of Lincoln County. Our thanks to both for their kind permission to use this work.

ISBN 978-0-9849588-8-7

Library of Congress Control Number: 2012942003

Printed in the United States

BELLE ISLE BOOKS
www.belleislebooks.com

To Mary Ann
and
In Memory of
Dr. James R. Winkler, DDS
1937-2008

CONTENTS

FOREWORD

———————————

Hard to believe, but I find today that well over half a century has passed since I began writing about the explosion of civil disobedience and violence that became known as the Lincoln County War. In articles, books, at seminars and supper tables, I have throughout those years voiced my conviction that no history of that "war" and/or the legendary life of Billy the Kid can be considered complete without a serious examination of the part played in it by the downtrodden and ruthlessly exploited Hispanic population of Lincoln County. As the author remarks, "nearly all the histories brush past any heroics by Hispanics."

But not this one. That its subject should be the life and death of Juan B. Patrón is—to me at least—a brilliant, much-needed step in the right direction. I remember my early mentor, Colonel Maurice G Fulton, extolling Patrón as a fine example of the very best kind of Hispanic citizen—only eighteen years old when he became a teacher to the town's children, then probate court clerk (the probate judge was Lawrence G. Murphy!) and eventually Speaker of the House of Representatives. That this man of the humblest Hispanic origin achieved so much in his life during those turbulent years is a close to astonishing achievement.

The story told here presents "the other lifestyle" never mentioned elsewhere, the way the work was done, the way the food was cooked, the way the children were raised, the primitive facilities that were all they had; it has understanding and respect and with admirable research offers the reader a great deal of new material and—perhaps its most valuable achievement—the fullest and most reliable account of Juan Patrón's mysterious death.

The author gently corrects a comment I made twenty years or so ago that there were no heroes in the Lincoln County War, and proposes that if anyone qualified, Patrón might very well be the one. Born in the most humble of circumstances, he became a leading figure among the Hispanic citizens of Lincoln, played a significant part in ridding the county of the Horrell clan in 1873 and just ten days before his 25th birthday won election to the Territorial House of Representatives in Santa Fe.

Refusing to take arms during the so-called war, he concentrated instead upon keeping the wheels of local government turning. Nonetheless, at the height of hostilities, and at some risk to himself, he gave shelter to Susan McSween and the Ealy family, and, at the behest of Governor Lew Wallace, formed and led the short-lived militia corps known as the Lincoln County Rifles—all but one of whose members were Hispanic—which helped bring a troubled peace to the county.

In 1879, Patrón moved to Puerto de Luna and married Beatriz, one of the daughters of Lorenzo Labadie, another influential Hispanic citizen whose life has been (until now) largely overlooked by historians. The author gives a detailed and long-overdue account of Patrón's by no means uneventful political career, and rounds it out with an impeccably detailed presentation—undoubtedly the fullest ever written—of the mysterious manner of his death in 1884, mapping out exactly what happened and offering some pertinent theories as to why Michael Erskine Maney, the man who killed him, never spent a day in jail and lived a long and comfortable life (he died in 1942 at the ripe old age of 84) without ever being required to account for or explain why he did it.

The picture of Juan Patrón that emerges here is largely that of a genuine, intelligent, honest, industrious man, but undoubtedly one with a dark strain in his personality. Even so, it is not too difficult to imagine that had he been born a decade or two later in a settled and more tolerant society, he might well have become New Mexico's first Congressman when statehood was conferred in 1912. This recognition of his achievements and premature death is long overdue, and I commend both it and its author to you.

Frederick Nolan
Chalfont St Giles, England

ACKNOWLEDGEMENTS

A score of published histories about violence in Lincoln County enabled me to set the proper stage for this book. Most notable are the excellent works by Frederick Nolan, Robert Utley and Mark Lee Gardner. To those authors and others noted in this book, I express my sincere thanks. I am especially indebted to Frederick Nolan for his foreward in the book.

This book also owes a large debt to many others. Most deserving of thanks is my good friend and fellow writer, Doug Wilburn, whose critical eye combed through the initial manuscript and brightened it. Also, his sleuthing spirit and that of Thalia Stautzenberger helped me piece together the life of Patrón's killer after his escape from jail. Heretofore, Michael Maney's whereabouts during the remainder of his life had been undisclosed.

Because Patrón's personal papers were lost in a shed fire after his death, I relied heavily on a small army of archivists and librarians who dredged for data that eventually fleshed out Patrón's story. These "unsung heroes" gave generously of their time and deserve high praise. They are Barry Drucker, former archivist at the New Mexico State Records and Archives; James Bradshaw, recently retired archivist at the Haley History Center; Laura Smith, archivist at the Santa Fe University of Art and Design; George Franchois, coordinator of library services at the U. S. Department of Interior Library; Karen Mills, historical records clerk for Lincoln County; Marina Ochoa, curator at the Catholic Archdiocese of Santa Fe; Tomas Jaehn at the Fray Angelico Chavez History Library, and Allison Deprey, collections assistant at the Indiana Historical Society.

Others who contributed in unique ways include Cleis and Jerome Jordan, who shared their Patrón collection while hosting my wife and me in the old Patrón home for several days; Herb Marsh, who escorted my small party to the canyon site of John Tunstall's murder; Fiorella Sanchez, who translated numerous documents in Spanish for me, Daniel Flores, who scoured church records and cemeteries to find certain marriage and death dates and Shelley Butler, who kept my confounded computer humming. To all of these friends, I express my deep gratitude.

Several Patrón descendants also deserve thanks for their support and for sharing family photographs and recollections. They are Charles Jones, Charles Munro, The Reverend William Sanchez, The Reverend John Brasher, Frances Aguilar and Francis Racel.

Writers need editors, and I was fortunate to have Annie Tobey assigned to me. With her seasoned eye, she suggested changes that gave the book greater clarity and readability.

Finally, I cannot begin to express the depth of my gratitude to my wife Mary Ann for her encouragement during the five years it took to develop and write this book. Throughout it all, she kept me on a steady course, endured my bouts of frustration and anxiety with quiet patience and consoled me with her gentleness. For that, I have dedicated this book to the love of my life.

INTRODUCTION

A Man for All Seasons

———————◆▸◈◂◆———————

I f one applied today's vernacular to history, Juan Patrón easily would
be viewed as the "go-to-man" during New Mexico's frontier days.
When urgencies demanded a courageous leader to defuse troubles in
Lincoln County in the 1870s, those around him turned to Patrón. Whether
asked to wield a six-shooter or a chairman's gavel, he always answered the
call. Three examples stand out. After the Horrell brothers shot up the town
of Lincoln, killing his father, Patrón secured a critical governor's reward
that sent the murderous brood scurrying home to Texas. Later, Governor
Lew Wallace trusted him to hold Billy the Kid in protective custody in a
specious deal the governor brokered with the Kid. Finally, when the army
refused Wallace troops to settle Lincoln's troubles, he turned to Patrón
again, directing him to organize and command Lincoln County's first
militia.

Yet nearly all histories about violence in Lincoln County brush past
any heroics by Hispanics. They center instead on the lives of desperados
like Billy the Kid or greedy Anglo merchants willing to kill for economic
dominance over a region populated mostly by Hispanics. This book is a
modest effort to correct that historical imbalance.

Patrón and most of his people wisely sat out the Lincoln County War.
Instead, they directed their energies toward good. While bullets flew all
around them, dirt-poor Hispanic farmers, who had defied the Apaches,
persistently tilled their lands and fed their villages. Despite the war and
threats on his life, Patrón kept a nascent government in America's largest
county, when judging by land size, functioning without any interruptions.

A respected historian correctly suggests there were no heroes in the
war. But if one looks to the sidelines, the real heroes were those Hispanic

and Anglo settlers who holstered their guns, kept their heads down and pushed forward in life without schools, churches, sanitation and doctors. In their struggle, they slowly paved a pathway toward New Mexico's statehood a century ago with modest achievements despite a litany of deprivation.

An important disclosure is necessary here. I am the father of four of Juan Patrón's great-grandchildren, having previously been married to one of his grandchildren. That being said, every effort was made to remain objective and true to history as I tried to resurrect the life of Juan Patrón from musty public records, newspaper articles and the private collections of personal papers. This is not the work of a historian but that of a former newspaperman who prayerfully has not betrayed the tenets of sound journalism. I introduce you to Don Juan Patrón.

CHAPTER 1

The Bishop and the Boy

I f ever a chunk of real estate embodied the wild American West, it was the Territory of New Mexico when it was ceded by Mexico to the United States in 1848. It was a raw frontier, rife with immorality and violence. Catholic priests passed their nights with dancehall girls. Feuds were settled with blazing guns, and a bottle of ninety-proof whiskey could ignite a drawdown over the slightest insult, be it intended or imagined.

The lives of two men, born nearly forty years apart on separate continents, eventually converged in this harsh, unbridled frontier, and through their own pursuits, they worked to tame it. Their beginnings were similar in some ways. Both men emerged from peasant families, benefited from Catholic schools and lost brothers and sisters to the rigors of early childhood. Their lives, however, ended in sharp contrast. One died peacefully in his sleep after a long life of religious accomplishments. The other was cut down by a Texas cowboy in a senseless saloon shooting at the height of a promising career in politics and business.

Jean Baptiste Lamy was the older of the two men, a French priest who came to America in 1839 when he was twenty-five years of age to serve as a missionary. Working in undemanding obscurity for eleven years, he established three busy missions in southern Ohio and in 1850 opened a new church as pastor of St. Mary's Parish in Covington, Kentucky, across the Ohio River from the bustling port of Cincinnati. Lamy's productive methods for acquiring land, creating new Catholic communities and raising money to erect new churches did not go unnoticed by his superiors in America.[1]

When the Vatican decided in 1849 that it wanted a spiritual leader to oversee its seventy thousand Catholics in the sprawling New Mexico

Territory, it tasked the bishops of America to submit a list of candidates. Meeting in synod in Baltimore in May of that year, the bishops settled on three candidates, listing Lamy first because of his "piety, honesty, prudence and zeal for saving souls" and sent their list of names to Rome.

On July 19, 1850, Pope Pius IX established the vicariate apostolic of New Mexico and four days later appointed thirty-five-year-old Father Jean Baptiste Lamy as its vicar apostolic with the title of Bishop of Agathonica. Receiving news of his appointment, Lamy sat amazed at his desk, wrestling with a bout of self-doubt about whether he was suited for the task. As letters of congratulations poured in from fellow priests, his confidence quickly lifted, and Lamy prepared for his journey to a land unlike any he had ever seen, a mixture of white desert sands, snow-capped mountains clad with pinon, cedar and pine and river valleys rich in grassy ranges.[2]

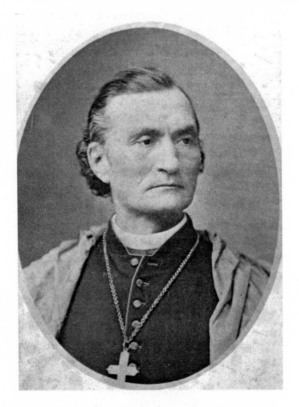

Bishop Jean Baptiste Lamy in 1870s

On November 24, Father Lamy took the short ferry ride from Covington to Cincinnati and climbed the hill to St. Peter's Cathedral, a massive Dayton limestone structure known among the clergy as the "bishop factory" for the past twenty-one bishops consecrated there. Inside the Greek Classical church, this humble French priest soon would become the center of a majestic and precise ceremony reaching back to St. Peter.

Trailing a long procession of priests, bishops and consecrators, robed in colored brocade vestments sewn with silver and gold, Lamy entered the grand cathedral and knelt between a pair of kneeling marble angels flanking the ornate altar. Thus began a three-hour ceremony, starting with an examination of faith, followed by the act of consecration and his investiture with all the regalia of his new office—pectoral cross, mitre, crozier, gloves and ring. Then Lamy read his oath as a new bishop, vowing his unflinching obedience to his Church.[3]

It was a dazzling moment for this unassuming priest, born of peasantry in a small clay farmhouse in the south of France. Lamy entered the world on October 11, 1814. Of eleven children born into his family, only four survived as adults. Two sons, Louis and Jean Baptiste, became priests, and daughter Marguerite entered the sisterhood. A third son, Etienne, fathered a son, Antoine, and a daughter, Marie, who in turn became a priest and nun. Antoine would later serve as a frontier priest under his uncle.[4]

Bishop Lamy set off for New Mexico in November 1850. After traveling for ten months by steamship, railroad, stagecoaches and mule wagons, Lamy and his trusted vicar general, Father Joseph Machebeuf, finally arrived in Santa Fe on Sunday, August 9, 1851. To their surprise, they were greeted by a throng of thousands, including the territorial governor and Monsignor Juan Felipe Ortiz, the ecclesiastical dean of New Mexico.

The afterglow of Lamy's jubilant welcome evaporated quickly the next day. Reflecting on his long journey across New Mexico, Lamy mournfully recalled that at every stop he had seen his beloved Church in general disarray and beset with moral and physical decay. Schools were non-existent. Of the fifteen priests available to serve parishes scattered across a land larger than France, six were so feeble they were inactive. The other nine priests either were too lazy to provide spiritual succor to the faithful or behaved scandalously, drinking, gambling and dancing with "carefree" women in local saloons.[5]

Thousands of Catholics—Mexicans and Indians—who inherited the faith, Lamy learned, were foregoing religious sacraments. They were unbaptized, unconfirmed and cohabitating outside of marriage and producing illegitimate children, simply because the clergy levied outrageous charges for pastoral services at birth, marriage, baptism and burial. "What," an exasperated Lamy asked an associate, "would you think of a priest who does not preach to his congregation but only once a year, and then on condition he will receive eighteen dollars?" In some cases, the exorbitant fees demanded by the clergy supported addictions to liquor and gambling. One old priest, while riding to a distant mission, was so drunk he fell off his horse and broke a leg in three places.

Still worse, priests openly betrayed their vows by indulging in adultery, some with live-in mistresses. Their behavior shocked visitors from the States. One layman observed, "The priests of New Mexico were noted for their corruption and profligacy, and instead of being teachers in morals they were leaders in vice. There was hardly a priest who did not rear a family of illegitimate children, in direct violation of his holy vows and laws of religion and morality."[6]

Most notable among the sexually active priests was Father Jose Manuel Gallegos, a popular pastor in Albuquerque. Vain and pretentious, he was the convivial crony of politicians and lived openly with a married Mexican woman, who had been the mistress of two Mexican officers in turn, by whom she had three children. With her money, she and Gallegos operated a general store that they kept open on Sundays in violation of church rules. Gallegos's behavior was so reprehensible, Lamy succeeded in removing him from the church.[7]

The vicariate Lamy inherited could not have been in a worse way. Illiteracy was widespread. Less than half of his Catholics could read their catechisms or sign their names because there were no public or religious schools. It was the ugly legacy of government policies imposed first by Spain and then Mexico to keep the populace ignorant and in peonage. Lamy faulted the priests and their previous superior, the bishop of Durango, Jose Antonio Zubiria, for the deplorable situation facing him. Bishop Zubiria, based fifteen hundred miles away in Mexico, had visited the New Mexico sector of his diocese only three times in twenty years. Lamy had a plan to fix his broken and neglected Church.

Lamy's first concerns were education followed by reformation of an errant clergy. "The state of immorality in matters of sex is so deplorable that the most urgent need is to open schools for girls under the direction of the Sisters of Charity," Lamy advised his financial supporters in France. He asked for fifteen thousand francs to open the first school and told of his plan to have a school for boys in each of his twenty-six parishes. Boys were being raised without being taught to respect female chastity. As a result, both boys and girls generally were promiscuous. Most appalling to Lamy was the common practice of parents selling their daughters into sexual servitude to older men, either through cohabitation or marriage.[8]

Life in the rural reaches of Santa Fe had not changed much since the days of the Spanish conquistadors. "Mexicans" and a few Anglos farmed in the valleys and on the plains. Although everyone called them Mexicans, they were Hispanic native New Mexicans who had lived there for generations. Their farming methods were handed down from past generations. The soil was tilled with a wire fork bound to a log and drawn by mules. In the canyons and on the mesas, they grazed sheep and ran goats, which they used for both meat and milk. They farmed "as the ancients did," one new arrival observed. "They tramp out wheat with sheep or goats, fan it by the wind and keep their guns tied to the plow beam."[9]

Such was the grim life facing a boy named Juan Bautista Patrón, the son of peasants, unable to read or write English and doomed to work long days in the fields, helping his family scratch out a living from a small patch of land. Luckily for this boy, Bishop Lamy opened his first schools in Santa Fe just in time to rescue his future.

Juan was the third of five children born to Isidro and Felipa Martinez Patrón. Born on November 20, 1852, he was christened with the same name of the Patrón's first son, who died shortly after birth in 1850. The family lived in a squat adobe house close to a stream that irrigated its small farm outside of Santa Fe. Juan's older sister Juana was born on November 29, 1845, and a younger sister, Encarnacion, on March 29, 1856. A younger brother, Sivoriano, died in 1860 before he was one year old.[10]

One month after Juan's birth, Bishop Lamy opened his first school, a convent for girls called Our Lady of Light. Run by the Sisters of Loretto, the convent welcomed its first girls, comprised of ten boarding students and twenty-two day students. Nearly all were from poor families. These young pioneers faced a hefty curriculum that would stand as a model for the boys' schools soon to follow.[11]

During a ten-month academic year, the girls delved into a host of core subjects, taught in English and Spanish. These included reading, writing, grammar, arithmetic, geography, history and orthography (spelling). The more advanced students also studied astronomy (with the use of globes), natural philosophy, botany, painting and French. Lessons in singing, piano and guitar were available for established monthly fees.

While the Sisters of Loretto were opening young minds to a world far beyond scruffy Santa Fe, Lamy received unexpected good news from Rome. Pope Pius IX had elevated Santa Fe to full status of a diocese on July 29, 1853, empowering Lamy with complete religious authority over his rebellious clergy. It gifted to Lamy the leverage to demand obedience from his clergy or face expulsion from the priesthood. Henceforth, he expected them to honor their religious vows by abandoning sinful practices and disavowing any loyalty to Bishop Zubiria in faraway Durango.[12]

Catholics in Santa Fe greeted Bishop Lamy's girls' school with enthusiasm. They rushed to send their daughters to Our Lady of Light. As enrollments grew, so did the convent, enlarging its classrooms and grounds every few years to accommodate more students. By 1865, the convent was attracting girls from families able to pay their way. Mother Superior M. Magdalen described the convent, its character and curricula in a newspaper advertisement that year:

> *CONVENT OF OUR LADY OF LIGHT*
> *This institution is under the direction of the Most Rev. Bishop John B. Lamy.*
> *The establishment for the education of Misses, is located in the most beautiful part of the city. The building is commodious and is surrounded by a large garden which affords ample room for the scholars to take exercise in.*
> *The culture of the intellectual faculties of youth and the training of them in the paths of virtue, being the important duties confided to the Sisters, they will take every care to instruct their pupils in those branches which constitute a useful and refined education, and above all, in the principles of the Catholic Religion and the duties which it imposes.*
> *The discipline is mild and parental, and at the same time strict and positive. The Sisters will take particular care of the health and welfare of scholars.*[13]

After five years, Lamy had succeeded in establishing schools for boys and girls in every parish. For these new students, their scholarship was as challenging as that demanded in the convent. In addition to their core subjects, students were instructed in ancient and modern languages, drawing, music and other subjects useful in "polite education."

CHAPTER 2

Education of Juan Patrón

B y 1859, Santa Fe had two hundred boys and girls enrolled in school, including seven-year-old Juan Patrón. Juan's father Isidro, having spent a lifetime in the fields, had ambitions for his son that went beyond the calloused hands of a weary farmer. Since Lamy's boys' schools drew students from mostly poor families, Isidro applied on behalf of his son, and young Juan was admitted.[14]

From the very start, Juan showed a thirst for knowledge and took to his studies like a young pup lapping up water. He progressed through his elementary grades with ease, learning to read and write in English, bringing home a language foreign to his parents. Words especially fascinated him. He learned that when properly used, words could be powerful and influential—a lesson he carried into his later political life, becoming one of New Mexico's fine orators.

Besides English, the nuns and brothers taught him Spanish grammar, Latin, orthography, world geography, Spanish and American history, mythology and penmanship. Juan adopted a sweeping cursive as he mastered the art of composing essays with correct grammar and punctuation, a rare talent on the frontier. As for the arts offered him, he favored singing and learned to play piano.

In 1858, Lamy began his push to provide higher education for boys. Aware of the high level of education Christian Brothers provided boys in Europe, Lamy wanted the same for his New Mexico lads. After some ingenious negotiations, he succeeded in recruiting five Christian Brothers from France to start a boys' high school for boarders and day students in Santa Fe.

On October 27, five bedraggled missionaries arrived at Lamy's doorstep, tired and a bit frazzled from a harrowing crossing of the Southwest plains in a wagon caravan exposed to daily attacks by marauding Indians. After a day of rest and being well fed, the brothers took possession of a flat-roof adobe home on a choice site that the bishop had procured for them. The building was next to St. Miguel's Church, the oldest in Santa Fe and perhaps in the nation.[15]

The house was spacious enough but poorly fitted for a small school. Brother Hilarien, leader of the five French educators, later described it as a simple "adobe hut with four walls." Its furnishings consisted of five mattresses and five blankets for the brothers' bedding, two tables and a few benches. There was no kitchen so the brothers took their daily meals at Bishop Lamy's table.[16]

Despite their Spartan-like surroundings, the brothers immediately went to work and within a few days had the semblance of a schoolroom ready for young scholars. On November 15, classes began for the first six boarding students. A week later, the first daytime students were admitted. Enrollment in the first year eventually totaled seventeen boarders and fifty daytime scholars. Thus, St. Michael's College was formally launched, and Lamy's dream of a college preparatory school became a reality.

So pleased with having a boys' high school in its midst, the Santa Fe *Daily New Mexican* expressed its daily pleasure of seeing "the cleanly, joyous little fellows going and coming from the place where they receive the seeds of instruction, from which shall grow the future rulers, teachers and businessmen of New Mexico."[17]

By 1865, Santa Fe's Catholic schools had more than five hundred enrolled students. Among those was thirteen-year-old Juan Patrón, who joined one hundred other boys studying at St. Michael's College. Under tutelage of the Christian Brothers, young Patrón faced challenges in scholarly disciplines he never knew existed. For the first time, he designed equations in algebra, applied formulas for measuring geometric forms, identified chemical elements, composed essays and learned accounting.

With each new school year, Juan felt his small classrooms grow more crowded as new boarding and daytime students vied for seats around the classroom tables. To handle the swollen student body, two old buildings across the street from the adobe school were converted into classrooms and boarding rooms. They wrapped around a hard-packed dirt courtyard used for physical exercise and practice by the school's small marching band.

Tranquilino Labadie was one of the new boarding students who packed St. Michael's classrooms. Two years younger than Patrón, he was from a well-known ranching family in the Santa Rosa area. His father, Lorenzo Labadie, had served as an Indian agent and sheriff in three New Mexico counties before settling into sheep ranching fulltime. From their first encounter, Patrón and Labadie were drawn together by mutual interests. Both had a yearning for learning and absorbed their lessons with relative ease. Both also harbored ambitions to one day enter New Mexico politics and serve in government. It was the beginning of a loyal friendship that lasted a lifetime.

Both boys also displayed a strong devotion to their faith, earning each of them invitations to join Bishop Lamy for an occasional day in the country at his favorite retreat. It was a small two-room villa in the Tesuque Canyon three miles north of Santa Fe, containing a study and small chapel where Lamy said Mass, with his guest students in turn serving as altar boys.[18]

Lamy closely monitored the progress of exceptional students, always on the lookout for those with an aptitude for higher education. Patrón's academic record caught the bishop's attention, and Lamy eventually recommended him for admission to Notre Dame University. Patrón descendants believed Juan attended Notre Dame, but he never did. Patrón chose to make his way in the secular world of politics.

Juan Bautista Patrón in early 1870s

During Patrón's final year at St. Michael's, overcrowding became so great that the director of the school, Brother Domitian, declared the school and dormitory unsafe and threatened to close the school rather than expand it. Bishop Lamy, however, interceded and with editorial support from the *Daily New Mexican* successfully prevented the school's closing.

The next year, Brother Botulph replaced Brother Domitian and brought new energy to St. Michael's administration. Orders from his superior were explicit: "Go to Santa Fe and make it go." He immediately drafted a plan for erecting a large new classroom building that would make St. Michael's the citadel of higher education in the Southwest.[19]

Long after Patrón and Labadie left St. Michael's College, the old single-story adobe school they knew was demolished to make way for a two-story building with a mansard roof and tall cupola. Its demolition came in 1878, a few months after Patrón and Labadie came to Santa Fe to serve as officers in the New Mexico legislature. When completed, the new school stood as the tallest adobe building in the Southwest and cost nearly twenty thousand dollars.

Patrón and Labadie were among the first in a long line of distinguished alumni who became prominent in public life in New Mexico. St. Michael's also earned a reputation for producing eloquent speakers, as the *Daily New Mexican* noted in a 1912 editorial. "Very often, in legislature," it said, "when people have praised an especially forcible address, they have ascribed it to natural eloquence, when as a matter of fact, it was due to the careful training received from the Christian Brothers at Saint Michael's College." By all accounts, Patrón had distinguished himself as one of those eloquent and forceful orators in the house.[20]

Governor L. Bradford Prince told the same newspaper in 1914 that he once started to make a list of prominent men who had attended St. Michael's, "especially of the law makers, in constitutional conventions and legislatures, who had carried the St. Michael's spirit into the statute books," but put it aside, realizing the list "would be like a directory of territorial and state officials."

Tranquilino Labadie also distinguished himself in politics. He and twenty-one other St. Michael alumni served as members of the 1910 Constitutional Convention that enabled New Mexico to be admitted into the Union two years later. Labadie then went on to serve as a house member in the first state legislature.

St Michael's influence reached into all facets of New Mexico's society, from priests and doctors to military men and politicians. For Juan Patrón and those who followed him, St. Michael's College served as a beacon of learning that helped New Mexico join the rest of the world.

CHAPTER 3

A New Beginning

———————

I sidro Patrón was a forty-eight-year-old widower in 1870, when he decided to move his family from Santa Fe to Lincoln, seat of a new county in the southeastern portion of New Mexico. It was a daring decision for a man who was enchained to a piece of land passed down through generations. His fore bearers spent lifetimes scratching the tired land, each in turn eking out a meager living for their families. At the urging of his son Juan, now an educated young man, Isidro decided to break the generational cycle and sold his land.[21]

Their move to Lincoln marked a new beginning for the Patrón family. Isidro's wife Felipa had died earlier from a lingering sickness. Juan, at eighteen, recently was graduated from St. Michael's, and the sale of the family's land provided enough money to buy a replacement farm and open a small general store in Lincoln. For the Patróns, it was their first view of a world outside of Santa Fe.

Lincoln's pastoral setting stood in sharp contrast to Santa Fe with its jumble of run-down adobe buildings strung along narrow, crooked streets and its roistering denizens of gambling houses and saloons. The village stretched less than a mile along a single dirt road, compressed between the slim Bonito River on the north and timbered mountains on the south. Willows and cottonwoods flourished along the river's edges while clumps of pinon and juniper shouldered the valley on both sides. In the distance, the humpback Capitans cast a mountainscape of bluish gray.

Daily life centered within Lincoln's small plaza. Farmers spread their goods on blankets as buyers picked over their mounds of melons, chili peppers, onions and fruit. Occasionally, noisy men circled around cockfights, loudly rooting for roosters bearing their bets. Sundays brought sounds of music into the square as families gathered to join in dancing the fandango. Throughout, roaming animals barked, brayed and clucked amidst the villagers, creating a cacophony that gave life to the small village.

When the Patróns arrived in Lincoln, the village counted nearly six hundred residents. Most were Hispanics, some of them recent arrivals from the north, like the Patróns. They lived in flat-roof adobes along small tributaries flowing eastward to the Pecos, namely the Bonito and Ruidoso, which joined to form the Hondo. Most native settlers farmed along the Bonito to the west, while a few Anglos staked out farms and ranches to the east along the Hondo, having settled there after completing hitches in the army at Fort Stanton.

With its hundred cavalrymen and mighty cannon, Fort Stanton evoked a sense of security in the area, providing settlements protection against marauding Indians and giving the appearance of a peaceful countryside. The fort sat in the middle of a military reservation that dated back to 1855. Located nine miles west of Lincoln, it stretched eight miles along the Bonito and extended one mile on each side of the river. Aligned in precise military order, the officers' quarters, soldiers' barracks, offices and stores formed a square, enclosing a parade ground, where the national flag floated from a tall flagstaff in the center.[22]

Lincoln served as the seat of government to a county in its infancy. Established in 1869 and named after a fallen president, Lincoln County sprawled across thirty thousand square miles, containing only three thousand people and tens of thousands of cattle. Nearly the size of South Carolina, it was the largest county in the United States and faced a shaky start, having required two elections to seat its first civil officers on April 19, after its first election in March was voided because of irregularities.[23]

The Patróns settled into a modest twin-peaked adobe in the heart of Lincoln, enjoying a tranquil life in their newly adopted town. With two front entrances, the house proved to be ideal. One doorway led inside to the family's living quarters and the other into spaces for a combined general store and saloon. The rooms inside were plastered with the native earth and whitewashed. To keep the whitewash from rubbing off, calico covered the walls to above shoulder height with mirrors and pictures hung above the calico. Bleached muslin stretched across the overhead beams to keep the earthen roof from powdering down. In a corner of the main room, a small, hive-shaped fireplace fueled with pungent piñon wood provided warmth and a place to cook.[24]

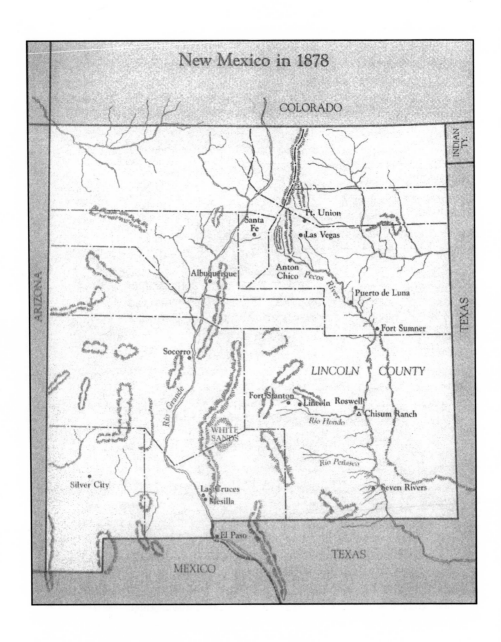

New Mexico in 1878

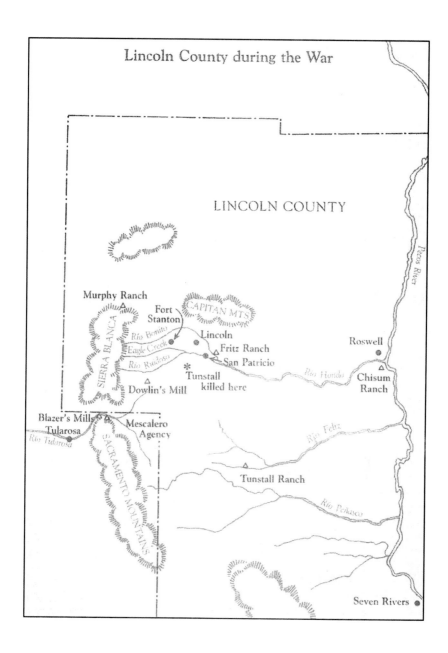

Lincoln County during the War

Juan Patrón house (left) and store in 1920s

While Isidro farmed on his small patch of land, Juan clerked in the small family store when he wasn't needed to help in his father's fields. Twenty-five-year-old Juana, the older of two daughters, managed the household, assisted by her fourteen-year-old sister Encarnacion, who adored her older brother and considered him her best friend. Tall and well framed, Juan had developed into a handsome young man. His soft brown eyes, firm chin and high cheekbones formed a pleasant face, capped by thick, black wavy hair.

As devout Catholics, the Patróns landed themselves in a county nearly devoid of places to worship. With no church in town, Catholics depended on three widely scattered small chapels to practice their faith whenever a priest was available. Padre Francisco Boucart, a French priest, made monthly visits to each chapel to offer Mass and perform baptisms and marriages. No stranger to the area, Padre Boucart first performed baptisms for settlers along the Bonito as early as July 1868, recording the first entries in what would become the Lincoln County parish book.[25]

When able, the Patróns worshipped at the Chapel of Rio Bonito, located six miles west of Lincoln and owned by a rancher, Antonio Torres y Marquez. At the time, it was not uncommon for a layperson, or even a priest, to own a chapel and related cemetery. A second chapel of St. Patrick stood on a corner of Anicito Lucero's ranch, twenty miles southwest of Lincoln on the Rio Ruidoso. Farther away to the east was an oratory dedicated to St. Joseph, a one-room sanctuary inside a private home in a village on the Rio Hondo.

From this small foothold in Lincoln County, the Church found itself competing with the barbarous *Penitentes* for the hearts and souls of fifteen hundred Catholics in the area. A renegade society of Catholics, the Penitents practiced mutilating rituals of atonement first introduced in Mexico and South America in the early seventeenth century. In atoning for their sins, the Penitents sought God's forgiveness through self-flagellation, carrying heavy crosses and binding the body to a cross so tightly it reduced blood circulation to the limbs.

Initiates into the society endured tests of extreme pain. After three perpendicular incisions were carved onto a candidate's back two inches below the shoulder, the inductee began a ceremony of wild self-thrashing with cactus whips. Initiations were held only during Holy Week, and on Good Friday it was customary to bind one of the brethren to a cross, as an enactment of a crucifixion.[26]

When Bishop Lamy tried to disband the society, it went underground and held its bloody rituals secretly in *moradas*, usually small adobe homes of its leaders. An intrepid reporter for the Las Vegas *Daily Optic* sneaked into a secret initiation of three candidates during Easter week in 1884 and later wrote this bloody account:

> At a signal from a man dressed in a long black gown, the three men arose, and each man picked up a long club-like apparatus made of soap weed and cactus burs wrapped around a rope, until it was about three inches thick. Holding their clubs in both hands, the three victims whipped themselves over their shoulders right and left, making the blood spurt and run in a dozen streams down their clotted and dirty backs.
>
> Led outside to a wooden cross, the three men, who had lashed themselves probably five hundred times, were almost fainting from loss of blood and excruciating pain when they were ordered face down on to the ground. The night was bitter cold, and the three victims shivered as if they were shaken by machinery. The elder then approached them and administered each about twelve hard, brutal lashes with a similar but larger club.

At that point, the sight of blood pouring from torn flesh overcame the reporter as he quickly departed "sick at heart and stomach."

When the Patróns came to Lincoln, the *Penitentes* were at the height of their popularity in New Mexico, as evidenced in a cemetery two miles west of Lincoln where thirty-one Penitents were buried, including women members known as *Carmilitas*. The society remained strong among all classes, despite demands by ecclesiastical authorities to abolish its rituals. Bishop Lamy's repeated efforts to disband the society only sent the renegade Catholics deeper underground.[27]

Given his Catholic education, Juan Patrón abhorred the rituals of the *Penitentes*. From his first days in Lincoln, he vowed to one day build a church in the town, confident that an active parish and church would suffocate the *Penitentes'* appeal to Lincoln's illiterate Hispanics. Patrón saw an opportunity to keep that promise in 1876, when he joined a local priest's campaign to raise money to build a church in Lincoln.

Lincoln not only had no church, it had no school. With youthful energy and the tools of education, Patrón opened a classroom in his family home, becoming Lincoln's first schoolteacher. Daily, a handful of boys circled around their eighteen-year-old schoolmaster, reading their first words of English and Spanish, scrawling simple sentences in shaky cursive and mastering basic mathematics. Like the Christian Brothers who led him out of the darkness of illiteracy, Patrón hoped to salvage the youth and enlighten their future.[28]

Patrón's students came from both Hispanic and Anglo families. He strived for them to learn each other's languages, hopeful it would foster cultural understanding and friendship among his small group of students. As the months passed, Patrón's role as a teacher endeared him to the families whose children benefitted from his free instruction.

As his popularity and standing in the community grew, so did his taste for politics. Nearly two years after arriving in Lincoln, Juan Patrón decided to become a candidate for probate court clerk of Lincoln County in the November 1871 elections. When voters cast their ballots, Patrón's beneficence as Lincoln's teacher was not forgotten. At age nineteen, Patrón stood victorious in his first run for public office.

CHAPTER 4

Violence Comes to Lincoln County

＊◦＞∗＜◦＊

J uan Patrón's journey into politics soon introduced him to the corrupt world of Lawrence G. Murphy, the preeminent citizen of Lincoln County. As probate judge, Murphy held the most powerful office at the county level. An Irish immigrant in his early forties and veteran of two regular army enlistments, Murphy headed the area's biggest mercantile business, known simply as "The House."

Major Murphy came to Fort Stanton at the close of the Civil War with another Civil War officer, Emil Fritz. When their enlistments ended in 1866, the two bachelors formed a partnership, and L.G. Murphy & Company became the post trader at the fort. As the partnership prospered, Murphy built an impressive eighteen-room trading post just outside the western edge of the fort and opened a small branch store with a saloon and rooming house in Lincoln. From these two locations, the company served both military and civilian customers.[29]

When Patrón joined Murphy in sharing probate court duties, Murphy already ruled the civilian economy and political life in Lincoln County. His power rested on federal contracts to supply beef, corn and flour to Fort Stanton and the Mescalero Apache Indian Agency at the fort. To fill the contracts, Murphy bought virtually all of the crops of surrounding farmers and paid for them with credit from his store instead of with cash. By fixing the prices both of buying and selling, Murphy controlled the cashless exchange, which always ended in his favor. "They intimidated, oppressed and crushed people who were obliged to deal with them," one citizen said of Murphy and his partners. "They were a gigantic monopoly." Farmers had nowhere to turn but to Murphy since small merchants like the Patróns and Jose Montano offered no market for their crops.[30]

Ranchers fared no better than farmers. By fair means or foul, Murphy drove ranchers into debt as well. When their credit ran out and high interest loans fell behind, he foreclosed on their land and resold it at exorbitant prices to unwary newcomers without benefit of legal title. As the vicious cycle kept turning, Murphy profited.

The army was not immune to Murphy's cynical manipulations either. In 1869, Murphy began bolstering his gains from federal contracts by falsifying vouchers, over counting Indians, inflating average beef weight and applying other fraudulent methods. He regularly bought stolen cattle at cut rates from outlaw gangs and renegade Indians and resold them to the government at full price.

Lawrence G. Murphy (seated) and James J. Dolan

Murphy's master of deceit was a new hire and eventual partner named James Joseph Dolan, another Irish immigrant and army veteran. Standing five feet three inches, Dolan had served as a clerk at Fort Stanton and had been a drummer boy in the Civil War. At age twenty, he was the antithesis of Murphy in stature and nature. Murphy was above average height, slender, balding and dull eyed, while Dolan was slightly built, bore a mouse-like face, with blue eyes and a cap of thick, black wavy hair. Murphy's affable nature and benign countenance masked an unflinching ruthlessness, whereas, Dolan was restless, hot-tempered and unabashedly menacing toward enemies. Men who stood up to them and their hired guns courted disaster. "If they couldn't run a man out of the country," one citizen explained, "they would bring about his death at the hands of henchmen."[31]

As the only Republican officeholder in the county, Patrón clashed often with Murphy, who controlled the Democratic Party in a staunchly Democratic county. In February 1873, the killing of two Hispanic ranch hands set off a fury in Lincoln. The two men worked on John N. Copeland's ranch. When one of them ran off with a pair of Copeland's "matched horses" and a new saddle owned by his neighbor, John H. Riley, Copeland chased down the thief and shot him dead on the spot. Later, the two ranchers began marching the dead man's partner toward Fort Stanton's guardhouse as they rode behind. Two miles into the march, the worker bolted through a thicket of scrub oak and ran about forty yards. When he refused to stop, bullets flew out of both ranchers' Winchesters, and the runaway dropped dead.[32]

The next day, Copeland and Riley rode into Lincoln and reported the killings to Probate Judge Lawrence G. Murphy, expecting exoneration since Riley was The House's major supplier of cattle. Juan Patrón, in his second term as probate court clerk, demanded they be arrested, pending a grand jury investigation. Copeland and Riley scoffed at Patrón's demand, arguing that they could not be arrested by a clerk without due process. While Judge Murphy demurred, an angry crowd of Hispanics began to gather outside. Fearing that the mob intended to lynch them, Copeland and Riley ran out to their horses and galloped toward the safe confines of the fort.

Armed with a warrant with only his signature, twenty-one-year-old Patrón was determined to bring in Copeland and Riley. He spent the remainder of the day recruiting a posse later described by the Santa Fe *Daily New Mexican* as "eleven of the worst men in the whole country, known thieves and murderers." The group included three local toughs, namely Lucas Gallegos, Manuel Lucero y Romero and Juan Gonzales, once described by a Fort Stanton commander as "a notorious scoundrel and cutthroat." The three Hispanics silently vowed to kill Copeland and Riley.[33]

The next morning, the Patrón posse left Lincoln for the Copeland ranch, about twenty miles away. The men were "armed to the teeth" with rifles, pistols, knives, some having as many as three pistols, according to the *Daily New Mexican*. Reaching the ranch at about noon, Patrón and his men charged the house with their guns drawn and cocked, only to find that Copeland had found a safer haven elsewhere.

To their surprise, Riley met them at the door. Patrón ordered Riley to lead the way on foot to his own ranch, a short distance away. Befitting an unruly band of toughs, the party helped themselves to feed for their horses and took over a meal that had been prepared for Riley and his men. They upended the Riley household, verbally abused him and ranted for a lynching when a young Fort Stanton officer happened by and cooled the possemen down—but not for long.

Soon after, and to the surprise of everyone, Copeland showed up at the Riley home. Patrón directed the two ranchers, both on foot, to lead the mounted posse to the body of the man Copeland killed. In the company of the young Fort Stanton officer, Lt. Argalus G. Hennisee, Copeland and Riley walked to the spot. "On arriving where the body lay," the *Daily New Mexican* reported, "Lucas Gallegos, puting (sic) a cocked pistol to the head of Riley asked 'You shoot that man?' Mr. Riley replying in the negative (said) he did not shoot." Patrón quickly interceded, calming Gallegos and the others. He wanted bloodless arrests, not vengeful murders.[34]

While Riley and Copeland stood worrying about their fate, several of Patrón's men dismounted to bury the body. As luck would have it for Copeland and Riley, an army detachment came over a rise and in sight just as the burial was done. Led by Capt. Chambers McKibbin, commander of Fort Stanton, the soldiers had been alerted by Dr. H. G. Tiedemann, a Lincoln surgeon under contract to the army. Tiedemann had been at Copeland's ranch when the Patrón gang arrived and, sensing danger, made a riding dash to the fort for help.

Faced by Capt. McKibbin and his armed troops, Patrón wanted no confrontation with the army. He had no choice but to give up bringing in the two killers. Riding with McKibbin was former sheriff William Brady, another Murphy minion whom the *Daily New Mexican* identified as a "United States Commissioner." Under Brady's questionable federal authority, Patrón and his men were arrested and escorted back to the fort.

Brady conducted a hasty "investigation" that exonerated Copeland

and Riley while Patrón and his men sat locked in the guardhouse until their bail could be posted. A Lincoln County grand jury later indicted Patrón for issuing illegal arrest warrants for Copeland and Riley, but the case was never prosecuted.

When Copeland and Riley went free after killing the two workers, tensions mounted between the Hispanics and Anglos in the county. New settlers upended old farming traditions, creating new frictions. Native farmers, who depended on upstream water, lost crops and irrigated land as new Anglos settled farms upstream and, without regard to their neighbors, diverted precious water vital to downstream crops. Angered at being disparaged by their Anglo neighbors and gunned down with impunity, Hispanics fought for their rights.

In May, a group of Anglo farmers built a dam and ditches to irrigate their croplands upstream from Tularosa, where the most militant Hispanics lived and farmed. When levels of their irrigation water began falling sharply, a band of downstream farmers stormed the Anglos' waterworks and destroyed it. When the Anglos tried to repair their dams and ditches, the Hispanics drove them away with gunfire.

Known as the Tularosa Ditch War, the conflict lasted a week with intermittent violence between the Anglos and a small band of Hispanics led by Padre Pedro Lassaigne, a French priest in his mid thirties. Based in Tularosa as pastor of the Lincoln County diocese, Padre Lassaigne empathized with the farmers' plight and took up their cause, earning a reputation as "an agitator" at Fort Stanton. At peril of being shot, he tried to block the advance of Fort Stanton cavalrymen into town but stepped aside when Captain Chambers McKibbin, the troop leader, threatened to hang him if his men were fired on.[35]

In September, Hispanics leveraged their majority in Lincoln County and carried their fight to the ballot box. In elections for county offices, Jacinto Gonzales defeated William Brady as probate judge. Juan Patrón was returned to office as probate court clerk. Manuel Gutierrez was elected justice of the peace and Juan Martin was elected constable. Although Jacob L. "Jackicito" Gylam, a loyal Murphy man, was elected sheriff, civil authority in Lincoln County was largely in the grip of Hispanics for the first time.[36]

CHAPTER 5

Isidro Patrón Killed in the Horrell War

If one were picking poster boys for Texans who harbored total disdain for people of Mexican descent, the Horrell boys would win the honor. A mean, rowdy band of five brothers, they drank whiskey with reckless abandon and yanked out their shooting irons at the slightest provocation. They considered Hispanics subhuman, referred to them as "greasers," and killing one didn't rate a notch on a Texan's gun.[37]

The Horrell brothers—Samuel, Martin, Thomas, Ben and Merritt—came to Lincoln County in September 1873 on the run from the law in Lampasas County, Texas. An angry posse chased them out of the Lone Star state after they had killed five Texas state policemen in a saloon gunfight the previous March. With all of their wives and children in tow, except for Ben's family, the brothers eventually settled in Lincoln County.

Together, the Horrell boys established a cattle ranch on homestead land at the mouth of Eagle Creek on the Ruidoso. To bolster their meager herd of cattle, they stole unbranded cattle from neighboring ranches. The Horrells were well known for "the branding, killing and skinning of other folks' cattle," said a rancher who knew them, "and they were loaded for bear, sober or drunk."[38]

It didn't take long for the Horrells to bring deadly trouble to Lincoln. On December 1, Ben Horrell, the second youngest of the brothers at age twenty three, and two Texas cronies, Dave Warner and Jack Gylam, the new county sheriff, spent the day marinating their brains in ninety proof Pike's Magnolia. At the point of feeling bullet proof and with the law at their side, the boys began shooting up the town.[39]

When confronted by Constable Juan Martin and ordered to give up their weapons, the three drunks spit at this order from a "damn greaser" and threatened to kill Martin. Then they stumbled down the street toward the local whorehouse, shooting in all directions along the way. At Martin's bidding, Juan Patrón and four other local men joined the constable and trooped to the brothel after Horrell, Warner and Gylam.[40]

Inside the house, Horrell and Warner were being entertained by two of the prostitutes when Martin confronted them. Backed by Patrón and the others, the constable said he was going to bring the two in for shooting up the town. Horrell and Warner resisted, and one of them fired a shot that killed Martin. Patrón and his men returned fire. The fusillade killed Warner but only wounded Horrell, who with Gylam burst out of the house and ran for cover.[41]

Patrón and the others—reportedly local tough Juan Gonzalez, Seferino Trujillo, Jose Montano and Joe Haskins—chased the two runaways and caught up with them down by the Bonito. Badly wounded and on his knees, Horrell begged for his life. His plea was met with a blaze of gunfire. "The Texans were murdered in cold blood," Maj. John Sanford Mason, commander of Fort Stanton, later reported to his adjutant general on Christmas Day. Horrell lay dead with nine bullet holes in his body. Gylam's body was riddled with thirteen wounds.[42]

Seething over their brother's murder, the Horrells rode into Lincoln the next day and demanded that the killers be arrested. They were told no arrests would be made because the three Texans resisted arrest. Infuriated, the Horrell brothers galloped back to their ranch, vowing reprisals against Ben's killers. Two days later, Seferino Trujillo and an unidentified Hispanic were found dead on or near the Horrell ranch. The Texans disavowed any involvement in the murders. "Accounts differ," Major Mason reported to his superiors. "Some say it was supposed to have been done by a herder in their employ. Others say that these Mexicans were found driving off cattle from the herd and were killed by the Texans."[43]

At this point, it didn't matter who killed the two Hispanics. War was escalating rapidly between the Horrells and Hispanic militants in the county. Major John Mason received intelligence that Padre Pedro Lassaigne had advised Hispanic partisans to surround and set fire to the Horrell ranch and "to kill the Horrells if they fled for the hills."[44]

On December 5, armed Hispanics gathered on Eagle Creek. They numbered forty men, including militants recruited from Tularosa by Juan Gonzales. Major Mason sent a small detachment of thirty men, led by Capt.

McKibbin, to encamp at the mouth of Eagle Creek, hoping to discourage the mob from attacking the Horrell ranch. Their presence failed to diffuse the situation.[45]

Sheriff Ham Mills was among those at Eagle Creek, giving the appearance of a legal posse, even though he held no arrest warrants for the Horrells. Mills owed his appointment to Lawrence G. Murphy, who handed him the sheriff's badge after Gylam's death. Since Mills wore the badge without benefit of election, his authority was questionable. Nonetheless, a warrantless Mills led his "posse" on a charge to the Horrell ranch.[46]

Armed and well fortified inside their house, the Horrells refused to surrender to Mills's authority. Despite the sheriff's presence, the Horrells knew that the posse's real leader was the feared and vengeful Juan Gonzales. The Horrells chose to fight off the invaders rather than put themselves at the mercy of Hispanic partisans. They had killed enough "greasers" to fear *ley de fuga,* the unwritten Mexican law of reprisal.

Watched from a distance by McKibbin and his detachment of soldiers, the two sides exchanged fire. Sporadic shots continued throughout the day while McKibbin looked on, constrained by army regulations forbidding military intervention in civil affairs. Despite the constraints, the detachment's presence had some positive effect. Eventually, gunfire between the two sides ended. Tired and frustrated, the Mills posse abandoned the bloodless fight and rode back to Lincoln.

Both Patrón and Frank Coe believed that the attack on the Horrells was a ruse engineered by Murphy to drive the Horrells out of the territory. "Murphy wanted the Horrells to flee the country," Patrón said, "so he could attach all of their property, such as cattle, lands and so on."[47]

During the next two weeks, a tenuous calm settled over Lincoln County. The Hispanics who had stormed the Horrell ranch dispersed. The Horrells went about their business with some brothers appearing in town for purchases at the Murphy store without inciting any violence. As Christmas approached, prayerful Noels pronouncing "peace on earth" were about to fall on flat notes in Lincoln.

The Horrell clan wanted vengeance as their pent-up anger over Ben's death boiled over. On the night of December 20, three of the Horrell boys—Sam, Merritt and Tom—rounded up a band of about twenty-five local Texans and galloped into Lincoln, looking for Patrón and the others who they believed killed Ben.

A Mexican wedding *baile* or dance was underway that wintry Saturday night. Inside a long adobe building known as Chapman's Saloon, the

Patróns gathered at a decorated table, greeting guests who had come to celebrate the recent marriage of seventeen-year-old Encarnacion Patrón. Tall, poised and striking in her colorful Mexican evening dress, Encarnacion stood on the arm of her new husband, Rafael Gutierrez, a twenty-five-year-old sheep rancher and part-time gold miner. The couple had been married two weeks earlier at Saint Rita Catholic Church in Carrizozo. After the celebration, the newlyweds planned to settle near Tularosa where Rafael and his father, Manuel, owned a ranch and home.[48]

Musicians began the festivities that evening, playing the traditional *La Marcha de los Novios*, or the "March of the Newlyweds," reserved for the honored couple. When the dancing began, single girls wearing brightly colored shawls, some chaperoned by their mothers, took seats along one side of the room, waiting for dance invitations by young men gathered along the opposite side of the hall. When a gentleman's dance invitation was accepted, he placed his hat on the young woman's seat to save her place, abiding by frontier etiquette. After the dance, the gentleman returned his partner to her seat and retrieved his hat.[49]

Gathered with the Patrón clan were their closest friends. Saturnino Baca, the most respected elder among local Hispanics, and his wife, Juana Maria Chaves, sat nearby, surrounded by several of their nine children. At fifty-three, Baca was responsible for naming Lincoln County while serving in the territorial legislature. Later, he would become county sheriff, and the Bacas would stand as godparents to two of Encarnacion's future children, an exceptional honor usually reserved for family members. Seated at another table were Jose Candelaria and his wife Pilar. Isidro and Jose farmed in adjoining fields, helping each other during harvest time. Isidro made friends easily, and he enjoyed their company. Unable to read or write English, he was learned in his native tongue and "known as 'The Professor' by his friends," his granddaughter, Ravitos Patrón Hinojos, said.

Near midnight, the dancing was winding down when the Horrell gang arrived outside the dance hall. Someone in the gang reportedly shouted, "Come on, we'll make them dance to our own tune," as they bounded down from their horses, drew their pistols and began firing into the building's windows.[50]

According to one account, the gang of avengers then burst into the dance hall, shot out the lights and began shooting randomly. "They wanted a Mexican by the name of Juan Patrón," Robert Casey said. "But he wasn't there, and they got his daddy. He looked a pretty good deal like him, and they killed him."[51]

Defenseless, the wedding celebrants dove for cover behind tables and chairs. When the shooting stopped, the Horrell gang thundered out of town, leaving behind a bloody carnage that included four dead men—Isidro Patrón, Isidro Padilla, Dario Balazan and Jose Candelaria. Wounded were Balazan's nephew and two women, Apolonia Garcia and Pilar Candelaria.

Suddenly thrust into the role of family head, a grief-stricken Juan Patrón tried comforting his two weeping sisters as best he could before joining other men the next day in burying the dead. When word reached Padre Pedro Lassaigne in Tularosa about the *baile* massacre, he set off on a fifty-mile buggy ride to Lincoln. Two days after the killings, he held a requiem funeral mass in Lincoln for the departed souls.[52]

The violent behavior of unruly Texans had driven Lincoln into a state of lawlessness. Days earlier, Justice of the Peace Manuel Gutierrez and Probate Judge Jacinto Gonzalez chose to flee town when Major Mason at Fort Stanton refused to intervene in maintaining the peace. Mason told them that his mission was to protect citizens from Indians, not Texans.[53]

With Gutierrez and Gonzalez hiding in the mountains, there was no civil authority to issue arrest warrants. Patrón feared that anarchy would descend on Lincoln if the Horrells continued attacks on Hispanics until they satisfied their revenge. He needed to get help in Santa Fe.

Leaving Padre Lassaigne behind to comfort his sisters, Patrón made a riding dash for Santa Fe to ask Governor Marsh Giddings to intervene. Known as a sympathetic friend of Hispanics, the governor often railed against the bigoted slurs used by Texans and soldiers. Sitting across from Giddings in the Palace of Governors, a young Patrón laid out his case, identifying the three Horrell brothers and their cohorts as principal attackers. Giddings agreed to intervene, promising a reward for each of the attackers. On his own initiative, he later wrote the secretary of interior about the bigotry. "There have several times come to me evidences of a strong prejudice on the part of soldiers against the Mexicans," he said. "Many of these Mexicans are as highly educated and as law abiding and intelligent as the large portion of the border Texans."[54]

On January 7, 1874, Governor Giddings issued a proclamation placing a one-hundred-dollar reward on the head of each of the three Horrell brothers—Sam, Merritt and Tom—and their two friends, Zachariah Compton and E. Scott. Even though names were misspelled in the proclamation, all concerned knew who the five men were. It was published two days later in the Santa Fe *Daily New Mexican*.[55]

On January 13, Lawrence G. Murphy called all Lincoln citizens to a mass meeting in which he succeeded in vacating all public offices except sheriff and had himself and two others named to a board to maintain order in town. As its chairman, Murphy was to be assisted by William Brady and Jose Montano. Another of his minions, James Dolan, was chosen as secretary to the board. Murphy effectively had set up an autocracy in Lincoln with a frightened citizenry temporarily turning over all civil powers to him and the board.[56]

Recognizing the Murphy board as a brazen grab for power, Governor Giddings declared it illegal before it could be put into effect. Juan Patrón later declared the "vigilante committee" had a more sinister purpose. "It was to dispose and get out of the way obnoxious parties...who have been opposed to their schemes and plots," he said. "The real object of the committee was to kill me and others."[57]

With a price now on their heads, the Horrells knew it was "open season" for any mob of "greasers" to hunt them down and kill them. On January 20, Sheriff Ham Mills assembled a posse of sixty Hispanics, including Juan Patrón, to arrest the Horrells. With arrest warrants in hand, Mills and his posse rode down the Ruidoso to the ranch where they faced a Horrell clan heavily armed and fortified inside their ranch house. Faced with the prospect of heavy bloodshed if they tried to bring in the Horrells, the posse instead drove off most of the Horrells' stock of horses and returned to Lincoln.

That night, the Horrell clan abandoned their ranch and drove themselves down the Hondo to Robert Casey's ranch and encamped there, about twenty-five miles southeast of Lincoln. The next day, the Horrells hired four men to move their remaining livestock, food and household items farther down the Hondo to Roswell. During the move, a band of Hispanics bushwhacked the movers and ran off with everything, without a shot fired.

Spurred on by a drunken L.G. Murphy, the Mills posse rode out again on January 25 to arrest the Horrells. This time, Murphy's partner, James Dolan, led the posse, but Patrón refused to be a part of the gang. Finding the Horrells gone, the posse burned down the ranch house, emptied the storage sheds of all the crops and corn and carried the loot back to Lincoln. Learning that their ranch lay in charred ruins, the Horrells declared war. They sent word to Lincoln that they intended to kill the men responsible for Ben's death and destruction of their ranch. Among others, Patrón now sat in their crosshairs.

Meanwhile, news reached Governor Giddings and District Judge Warren H. Bristol in Santa Fe that more lives would be lost unless the military intervened in what had become guerrilla warfare between the Texans and militant Hispanics hunting down the Horrells for reward money. To calm matters, the governor and judge decided to recall the warrants Bristol issued earlier for the Horrells's arrest and sent a letter to that effect to Sheriff Mills via Major Price at Fort Stanton. On January 28, Mills and Patrón set off for Santa Fe to return the unsatisfied warrants.

In the meantime, the Horrells began a slow ride from Roswell toward Lincoln, recruiting restless cowboys refreshing their herds along the Pecos before driving them north. Like the Horrells, these Texas cowboys delighted in killing "greasers" and by the time the Horrells reached Bob Casey's ranch on the Hondo, their gang had grown to more than fifty men. Along the way, the bunch is believed to have killed three Hispanics, for no given reason, about forty miles east of the Casey ranch.

Another killing by the Texas drovers epitomized their zeal for cold-blooded murder. Lily Klasner, a Casey daughter who was fourteen at time, recounted the incident in her memoir. When the Horrell gang reached the village of Picacho, near the Casey ranch, they went to a home of the Rainbolt and Akers families and demanded breakfast. One gang member, known as Edward "Little Hart," became impatient waiting his turn for breakfast and asked if an American family lived in a house across the Hondo. Told that an American and his Mexican wife lived there, Little Hart said in a casual tone, "We'll just go over there and kill the fellow for that." Then Hart and two other cowboys galloped over to the Haskins house. When they reached the door, they hollered out, "Hello!" and Haskins came out the doorway. Haskins hardly reached outside when Little Hart shot him dead while his wife Antonia looked out the doorway.[58]

"Little Hart and his two companions had never seen Haskins before," Lily Klasner said, "and they had no personal grudge against him." However, Hart unwittingly had settled at least one score for the Horrells. Haskins had been in the Patrón posse responsible for Ben Horrell's death.

Their bellies full from the forced hospitality of the Rainbolts, the Horrell gang continued its ride up the Hondo toward Lincoln. Within a mile of town, the Horrells stopped, reevaluated their plan and, with no explanation, decided against leading a killing spree through Lincoln. Reporting to his superiors later, Major Price believed the Horrells turned the gang around, fearing they could not control their reckless band of recruits from indiscriminate killing.[59]

With their ranch burned out, their crops and household items looted earlier by a marauding posse and a bounty now on their heads, the Horrell brothers turned their back on Lincoln for the last time. They decided to ride south along the Rio Hondo toward Roswell, gather up their families and move the clan back to Texas. However, their ride downriver turned into a bloody rampage by the Texans about fifteen miles west of Roswell. Lily Casey Klasner wrote in her memoir:

> [The gang] met six ox teams, five of which were driven by Mexicans, while the remaining one was driven by an American, George Kimbrell, who was married to a native woman. The Harrells [sic] immediately began shooting and killed all five Mexicans. George Kimbrell somehow managed to come out of this affair with his life, but no one ever clearly understood why, since he had a Mexican wife, he did not meet a fate similar to that of Joe Haskins.[60]

With Juan Patrón's help, Kimbrell later would become the first non-aligned county sheriff in the wake of the Lincoln County War.

Meanwhile, Patrón and Sherriff Ham Mills reached Santa Fe. On February 2, they met with Governor Giddings and Colonel John Gregg, the top military commander in the territory. In urgent tones, Patrón requested that soldiers be directed to maintain peace and order in Lincoln because civil authorities were powerless to do so. Unbeknownst to Mills, the Horrells had ridden off with all of his grazing stock the previous day.

Patrón and Mills described the dire situation in Lincoln County much like it had been reported in the Santa Fe *Daily New Mexican* on January 27, 1874. The newspaper report was based on a private letter it had received from Lincoln about the war between the Texans and the Hispanics:

> All here is war and rumors of war. A general distrust prevails throughout the whole section. Every man met is armed to the teeth. Up and down the Rio Hondo, a number of ranches have been deserted, and now many fine places can be purchased for a song, their owners and occupants being determined and anxious to depart from a place where the reign of peace and order will not apparently be established for a long time to come.

On February 5, Judge Bristol joined the call by Patrón for military intervention to restore order in Lincoln County. In a formal request to Colonel Gregg, the judge declared that open warfare in the county "has rendered civil authorities powerless" and that the territory "has neither the arms nor the means to equip the required force to quell the disturbances."[61]

All this wringing of hands in Santa Fe proved for naught. The Horrell clan abandoned New Mexico days before and were hell-bent for Texas. The "Horrell War" was over, and the citizens of Lincoln, who once cowered inside the town's stone tower or *torreon* in fear of the Texans, were able to go about their daily business. Fort Stanton recorded twenty-nine deaths resulting from the war but acknowledged more may have gone unreported.

Patrón and Mills returned to a peaceful Lincoln. On February 18, the new commander at Fort Stanton, Major David R. Clendenin, reported to his superior, Colonel Gregg, that Sheriff Mills had advised him that "he does not need Military assistance at present.... Everything seems to be quieted down. The Texans have left the county and the Harrolds (sic) are reported back at or near Fort Concho, Texas."[62]

Murphy had achieved his goal of running off the Horrells, acquiring their land, cattle and crops at little cost. Shortly after the Horrells fled, Murphy's company made an unrecorded claim on the abandoned Ruidoso ranch and later sold it, without legal title, to Richard M. Brewer.

Calm had temporarily returned to Lincoln, but racial tensions simmered just below the surface of daily life. "The people were divided into two parties," Patrón said, "the Mexican element standing behind me, and the Americans, soldiers and Murphy against me." By then, the one-time schoolteacher had become *el guia*, or guiding leader, of the county's native New Mexicans.[63]

CHAPTER 6

A Cowardly Shot

———◆◆◆◆◆———

After serving two terms as probate court clerk, Patrón decided in 1875 to spread his political wings and reach for higher office as the Republican candidate for a seat in the territorial house. By then, he had gained respect and popularity among both Hispanic and Anglo voters and was recognized as the leading Republican in the county. As he began mounting his campaign, Patrón suddenly found himself in political hot water.

In April 1875, a grand jury investigation revealed that $20,000 in tax collections went missing during the time Lawrence Murphy controlled the county treasury as probate judge. For years, Murphy treated the county treasury as his own account. "He handled all the money as he saw fit," said one citizen. Murphy escaped indictment by resigning, and Florencio Gonzalez, a former territorial assemblyman, won a special election to take over the probate bench.[64]

The same grand jury also delivered embarrassing news about failed tax collections. A territorial auditor told jurors that tax collection in Lincoln County was two years in arrears. As ex-officio receiver of taxes, Murphy explained to the jury that the non-collection of 1873 taxes occurred because former sheriff, Jacob L. Gylam, was killed in the Horrell War and thus unable to carry out his duty as tax collector. As for the 1874 taxes, Murphy explained, Apache raids upon area ranchers and farmers made it impossible for Sheriff Ham Mills to collect taxes safely.

The Jury found Murphy's explanations unacceptable and indicted four county officers for dereliction of duty: Mills, County Treasurer Jose

Montano, Probate Court Clerk Juan Patrón and Justice of the Peace Pablo Pino y Pino. In its indictments, the jury said that the loss of taxes stalled the building of a school, courthouse and jail.[65]

Most taxpayers in the county believed their taxes were being misappropriated regularly, but no one knew whom to blame with any certainty. In the summer of 1875, an anonymous Democrat, badly in need of good grammar, pointed the finger at Juan Patrón in a letter to the editor printed in the *Mesilla News* on August 18:

> Mr. Editor: When the Borderer newspaper come in this week I look in it and find the name of Juan B Patrón of Lincoln county the Democratic candidate for representative to the legislater. Now I reckon this the same Juan B Patrón what used to be the probate clerk of the county and the same feller what got kicked out of being Assessor of the county because he got cotched in swinlin the people, and the same man who was twice indicted by the Grand Jury at the last Court on account of his robbin the county and the same Patrón who has been doin the dirty work of the swindling ring that have been rulin Lincoln county and a disgustin of every honest man and democrat in the county.
>
> Now Mr Editor I don't hold to be much of a writer or a politicion, I always pays my debts and my taxes here in Lincoln county and the corrupt ring that rules this county has never paid a cent of these taxes that I work hard for, but has put the money in their pockets and the county and the Territory has got no benefits of it and thats what's the matter with Hanner and that's the reason a Grand Jury of good Democrats put inditements against Juan B Patrón for swindling the county.
>
> We got a mean thieving ring in this county what steals all the taxes, and the honest men here are tryin to brake it up and we don't want no Juan B Patrón because he's in with that ring and so far as his politics hes nothing but a Maverick anyhow. Patrón would be a radical in a minit if he think Juan B Patrón would make anything out of it.
>
> We did want old man Chisum rite bad to be our candidate, hes a square man and good man and a good democrat, but if we can't get him, dont take Patrón, take somebody else, take a bull calf that don't belong to no thievin ring and put this in your paper if you can read it and if you wont put it in for the sake of honesty, let me know and I pay you if I have to sell a cow.

It was probably wise for this grousing writer to remain anonymous to protect his own life since many of his accusations toward Patrón were subtle indictments of Murphy and Dolan. Calling them a "swindlin ring that have been rulin Lincoln county" couldn't have settled well with Murphy and Dolan, known for hiring outlaws to silence their most vocal critics.

This semiliterate letter writer also had his facts confused in several instances: Patrón was a well-known Republican, not a Democrat, and was his party's candidate in the race for a territorial house seat against Paul Dowlin, a Democrat hand-picked by Murphy. John Chisum, referred to by the writer, was known as the Cattle King of the Southwest and no friend of Murphy's. Lastly, no credible histories of Lincoln County ever placed Patrón within any corrupt ring in Lincoln County or Santa Fe. In fact, he was a fierce opponent of the Santa Fe Ring.

Charges against Patrón and the others for failing to collect the 1873 and 1874 taxes were never prosecuted. Some believed the jury's subtle intention was to serve notice that lax collections no longer would be tolerated by the people, and the threat of prosecution would result in earnest efforts to make future collections.

Just as racial tensions were easing, violence broke out again on Lincoln's main street. Juan Patrón was one of the victims, and the shooter was John Riley, another hot-headed Irishman and business partner in the Murphy-Dolan cabal.

John Henry Riley

On September 15, 1875, Patrón and Riley were seen arguing in the middle of the street in front of Sheriff Saturnino Baca's home. The cause of their dispute is unknown. Some believed it was sparked by an enmity between Patrón and Riley stemming from Riley's escape from prosecution in the deaths of two Hispanic ranch hands in 1873.

After Patrón's near-fatal wounding, Riley testified before Justice of the Peace John Wilson that Patrón had followed him around that day, verbally abusing him and eventually drew a pistol on him. At some point, Patrón turned away from Riley and instantly heard the crack of Riley's carbine. A hot ball plunged into Patrón's back, near the spine, and settled in the abdomen. Patrón fell facedown onto the dusty road, lying near death as Riley simply walked away.

The buckboard driver who carried Patrón to Fort Stanton for medical attention that day told the Mesilla *News* that Patrón was intoxicated. The shooting incident was the first public glimpse of Patrón's quarrelsome nature when drinking. It contrasted sharply from his usual congenial manner and mild temperament. However, excessive drinking by day and evening had become a widespread custom for most men in Lincoln and every other village in the territory. And as a saloon owner, Patrón had ready access to the frontier's two popular whiskies, Double Anchor and Pike's Magnolia.[66]

Justice Wilson accepted Riley's plea of self-defense, as inexplicable as it was since Riley offered no explanation as to how he came to shoot Patrón in the back if he supposedly was defending himself. "He was a damned coward," Frank Coe recalled, explaining that Riley was better known for "providing the dirt" for a fight but out of sight when the shooting started.[67]

Thanks to the well-trained hands of Army Surgeon Carlos Carvallo, posted at Fort Stanton, Patrón made a remarkable recovery, despite press predictions he likely would die from his wounds. Even though he survived Riley's cowardly shot, Patrón now faced life with a crippled left leg.

Patrón partisans believed that Riley purposely drew his enemy into verbal combat that day as a ruse ordered by Murphy to silence the fiery young politician. Well-educated and the undisputed leader of the Hispanic community, Patrón also had gained widespread popularity among Anglos for speaking out against The House's unfair pricing practices.

Another of Murphy's outspoken critics was Robert Casey, a stern army veteran and wealthy rancher who operated a busy gristmill ten miles east of Lincoln. His place also served as a social and economic center in that area. On August l, Casey and Patrón were leading a Republican convention to nominate candidates for local offices when Murphy, a Democrat, burst into the meeting. "Knowing the convention was opposed to him," Patrón said, "he overthrew the table, destroyed the stationery, and said, 'you might as well try to stop the waves of the ocean with a fork as try and oppose me.'"[68]

After the convention adjourned, Casey went to the Wortley Hotel for lunch. At his table sat William Wilson, an itinerant cowboy and former employee, who wanted to talk to Casey about eight dollars in back wages. Weeks before, Casey had hired Wilson on his wife's recommendation that she saw some good in the man. After lunch, the two men parted and Wilson quickly hid around the corner of a building across from the Wortley.

When Casey came out of the hotel, Wilson triggered his Henry rifle, and the slug shattered Casey's hip. Bent on killing Casey, Wilson pursued the wounded rancher as he tried to drag himself to safety. Wilson's rifle barked again, and the next shot tore into Casey's skull, near his mouth. Casey lay critically wounded on Lincoln's rutted dirt street. The next day, the scrappy frontiersman died.

Casey's murder occurred just six weeks before Patrón was shot in the back by Riley. Casey's family was convinced that Murphy hired Wilson to kill Casey and promised the former convict protection from the law. But Wilson was not as lucky as Riley after he shot Patrón. Wounded in the leg and captured in a thwarted escape attempt, Wilson went to trial and was found guilty of murder. On October 18, he was sentenced by Judge Bristol to be hanged.

Wilson's trip to the gallows on December 10 marked the first legal hanging in Lincoln County and is remembered also for its incredible moments. A large crowd gathered that day around the scaffold near the courthouse to witness the hanging. Patrón stood among the anxious onlookers. As a close friend of Casey's, he wanted to see justice delivered for the dead man's widow and their brood of children. While standing before the gallows, Patrón recognized the Catholic priest standing on the platform, preparing to deliver last rites to the condemned man. He hoped to talk afterwards to the young padre about his beloved uncle.[69]

As Wilson was led up the steps of the platform, waiting for the condemned man were Sheriff Saturnino Baca, in charge of the execution; Murphy, who had no official standing to be there; and Father Anthony Lamy, the twenty-nine-year-old nephew of Patrón's childhood mentor, Archbishop Lamy.

Based in Manzano, northwest of Lincoln, Father Lamy was at the execution merely by chance. While on his routine round of visiting villages along the Rio Bonito, the priest also stopped at Fort Stanton. At the fort, Lamy met with Wilson in his cell "and stayed with him for more than an hour giving him all the spiritual consolation in my power," he later wrote to his sister.[70]

After the death warrant was read to the on-looking crowd, Baca said he would allow Wilson to spend thirty more minutes with Father Lamy before the execution. When the crowd protested loudly, threatening to take matters into its own hands, Baca hastily began the execution.

After the trap door was set for triggering, Wilson was allowed to say his final words. He turned to Murphy and bitterly declared, "Major, you know you are the cause of this. You promised to save me but—." Hearing this, Murphy kicked the lever that triggered the trap door, and Wilson dropped through the opening like a let-go heavy anchor, his body dangling from a taut rope.[71]

After hanging motionless for nearly ten minutes, Wilson's body was taken down by Sheriff Baca and his helpers. Wilson was pronounced dead and placed into a waiting coffin. As the crowd began to disperse, a curious Hispanic woman lifted the coffin lid to peek inside and screamed loudly, "For God's sake! The dead has come alive!"[72]

Murphy tried to seize this moment of great confusion by declaring that since Wilson had been legally hanged, he could not be hanged a second time. Casey supporters in the crowd saw Murphy's declaration for what it was—a sly trick to spirit Wilson to safety and thus keep his promise to the condemned man.

Casey's friends, exasperated over the botched hanging, were determined to have Wilson hanged again. They procured a rope, tied it around Wilson's neck, dragged him from the coffin and strung the man's limp body up from the scaffold's crossbeam. After hanging in the air for another twenty minutes, Wilson's body was cut down and this time there was no doubt that the unfortunate man was dead. What started out as Lincoln County's first legal hanging effectively turned into an old-fashioned lynching.[73]

Father Lamy rode with Wilson's body in the army ambulance to consign it for burial and later went on his way. However, his brief time at Fort Stanton proved unfortunate. While there, the priest became exposed to the "fever," and he died on February 7, 1876, nearly two months after witnessing the execution of William Wilson. When told of his nephew's unexpected death, a saddened Archbishop Lamy ordered the bells of Santa Fe to toll that day for Anthony Lamy.[74]

CHAPTER 7

John Henry Tunstall Comes to Lincoln

E ven though Juan Patrón's stride was hobbled by his near-fatal wounding, it didn't slow his ascendancy in Lincoln County's politics. In the fall of 1876, Patrón declared his candidacy for a seat on the three-man Lincoln County Commission. As a commissioner, Patrón reasoned he could shield the county's treasury from the greedy hands of Murphy and Dolan. And running the largest county in the state provided a springboard in his ultimate quest for a seat in the legislature.

Five days before the November elections, Juan Patrón found himself busy in Santa Fe, more than a hundred miles away from the voters of Lincoln County. In late October, Alexander McSween, the county's only attorney, had asked Patrón to carry him in his buggy to Santa Fe on the lawyer's first leg of his journey to New York. On their arrival, McSween introduced Patrón to a young Englishman named John Henry Tunstall.

McSween, a Scotsman, had met the Englishman in a chance encounter weeks earlier in Santa Fe. The two spent an amiable few hours together, Tunstall eager to learn about the prospects of starting a stock-raising business in Lincoln and McSween touting Lincoln County in glowing terms for raising cattle on public lands unencumbered by Spanish land grants.[75]

McSween was ten years older than Tunstall. Considered handsome by some, he sported a youthful face topped by a thinning mop of curly black hair and a long bushy mustache drooping on each side of a firm chin. His dark eyes, often murky from the rigors of asthma, were set behind a perfectly formed nose. Always attired in a white shirt, tie and coat, he looked like a frontier lawyer.

Alexander A. McSween

The McSweens were relatively new to Lincoln, having arrived there on March 3, 1875, penniless and carried into town on a farmer's wagon. But they were determined to find their El Dorado. Alexander McSween believed fortunes could be made in Lincoln, and he quickly earned enough to provide the couple with stylish wardrobes and to begin drawing plans for a large new home.

On first meeting him, Tunstall judged McSween to be an able lawyer. He found the barrister to be ambitious, industrious, peacefully inclined and a non-drinker—traits similar to his own. The Englishman especially appreciated that McSween, like himself, detested confrontation and violence. One difference did exist between them. McSween swore never to carry a firearm, while Tunstall hid a single-shot Colt .45 under his coat. If he ever had to face a confrontation, Tunstall told his family in London, "I have contracted the habit of keeping my hands on my 'shooting iron.' It carries a fearful ball & shoots quick [sic], but I don't calculate to have to use it."[76]

After meeting this second time in Santa Fe, Tunstall and McSween went their separate ways. The lawyer left for New York City on behalf of a client, and Tunstall made plans to go to Lincoln. McSween had aroused the Englishman's interest with tales of opportunities for making easy profits in Lincoln. Ever since Tunstall's arrival in New Mexico, his hunger for wealth had become an obsession. He envisioned commanding a grand ranch with thousands of acres for grazing his stock. Within days, he was riding south in Juan Patrón's bouncing buggy.

John Henry Tunstall

Ever the prolific letter writer, Tunstall described his ordeal on the road with Patrón in a long letter to his parents in London. With the salutation, "My Beloved Trinity," referring to his father John Partridge Tunstall (the "much beloved Governor"), his "dearest Mama" and three sisters, the distant adventurer told how he often called upon a British stiff upper lip to deal with arduous moments on the long journey.

It began when Patrón called on Tunstall at about 9 a.m. on a Friday morning in a small hamlet named Galistea, a few miles south of Santa Fe, to begin the first leg of their journey, a forty-three-mile stretch to an overnight station. But the two men got off to a rocky start, as Tunstall reported in his letter:[77]

> It was snowing two days before this and the roads were like so much pudding. [H]ad I been traveling alone I should have been on the road about 6 a.m., but consistent with the imprudence of

the Mexican race, my friend Patrón was not ready to start until 10:30 a.m.

A Colonel [Saturnino] Baca (also a Mexican) and his brother-in-law were also traveling the same road and in company with us. They insisted that I ride in Patrón's buggy. Baca soon left us far behind and eventually got clear out of sight.

I don't like to wound your sympathies by describing the mental torment I endured during the next four days, but this vivacious history would be incomplete without it, so I will try to convey a little of it to your minds.

[O]ur horses were a couple of poor scarecrows that looked as if the harness must gall them all over. [O]ur buggy was heavily loaded, had no [brake] and the harness had no breaching. [T]he roads were heavy without compass and tolerably supplied with hills....

Patrón, for the first twelve miles (which he told me were the worst of the stage), flogged his horses along up hill and down and fairly exhausted them. [H]e never availed himself of the solid parts of the road, but went right along the ruts and mud, when half of the strength of the horses would have been saved by driving twelve inches to the right or left.

Tunstall quickly saw that Patrón was a wretched driver, for his fellow traveler held the reins so loosely that he had "no command of the team." When Patrón had to guide the team right or left, he wildly swung his hands either into his passenger's face or well into the back of the buggy. Several times, the Englishman politely suggested that Patrón tighten his reins and ease up on whipping the poor horses.

But it was no use, Patrón was everlastingly gazing at the horizon and flogging away at the horses spasmodically. The consequence of this was that when he stopped at noon, our near horse looked as if he would die in his tracks [and] he would not eat and could hardly move. The wind swept over the vast plain... like ice, and I was as cold as charity.

We hitched up the horses [after] about an hour and a half with the idea of starting [again], but the poor beast could not move. The only way out of this dilemma was for Patrón to ride on the other horse and come back for the buggy with either my horse or some other the next day.

We unharnessed the horses again and I, cursing the entire Mexican race from Patrón upwards and downwards, made up my mind to grin and bear it along the plains till next morning.

But an unexpected twist of fate came their way. While unharnessing the team, Tunstall accidentally let the sound horse loose, and it took the two men about an hour to catch him. In that time, the other horse, to their surprise, had made a remarkable recovery, good enough, they thought, to carry them six more miles to a small mud adobe home. When they reached the home, they received a "good meal before a good fire, which improved the aspect of things considerably" for Tunstall.

Eager to reach Lincoln and the comforts of a warm bed, the two pressed on deep into Sunday night, finally making camp alongside some Mexicans in a timber-combed hollow on the trail. For Tunstall, it was the most unbearable night of the journey. He described it in these words:

We had only two pairs of miserably thin blankets, no grub and the fire was so placed amidst the trees that it was impossible for both of us to be warmed by it. I gave up the warm side to Patrón. It was 3 a.m. [Monday] when we lay down, and I was nearly perished with cold till 6 a.m. when I arose.

I can't say I was much refreshed, and my breakfast...consisted of a large piece of bread as large as a halfpenny bun and five days old, with about enough butter to make a scanty accompany-ment to about half of it. It did not tend to reconcile me to my discomforts of the night before.

After the pair awoke, setbacks continued to plague their travel. When Tunstall and Patrón hastily made camp the night before, they believed their horses, badly drained from the day's sixty-five-mile haul, were too tired to wander very far from camp, so the men chose not to secure them. Tunstall's letter continues:

We were however mistaken, for they were nowhere to be seen. I walked about seven miles looking for them without success. [A]t last, our last night's neighbor fastened the pole of our buggy to the back of his wagon, and Patrón rode with him while I walked.... Patrón of course could not walk [because of his lame left leg] which he has very little control over.

After traveling about eight miles, they found their horses on the road, harnessed them and hurried toward Lincoln. .During their hapless four days along the trail, the two strangers came to know and appreciate each other. Even though Tunstall was quick to disparage Patrón's poor buggy handling, he did admire the New Mexican's intellect and character, writing,

> Patrón is a very good sort of fellow and the best educated Mexican I have met. [H]e is quite intelligent, appears to have good principles and certainly [is] kind hearted. [B]ut it was nothing short of agony to sit and watch him drive, or rather hold the reins, for no one could call it driving.

The two finally reached Lincoln at about 2 p.m. on November 6. Patrón hastily left his traveling companion to explore the small town on his own. The next day, voters were to choose a new slate of county officers, and Patrón went off to hustle votes for a seat on the Lincoln County Commission.

On November 7, voters cast their ballots, and Patrón easily won a seat on the commission. Also elected as commissioners were Will Dowlin and Francisco Romero y Lueras. As for the other county offices, James H. Farmer was elected Justice of the Peace and William Brady, a Murphy loyalist, was elected sheriff.

The new commissioners took their oath of office on January 23, 1877, and in a subsequent organizational meeting, Patrón was elected chairman.[78]

CHAPTER 8

Deadly Competition

W hen Juan Patrón brought John Henry Tunstall to Lincoln, the young Englishman found himself planted in a harsh land in sharp contrast to the posh London surroundings he had left behind in search of riches in America. As the only son of a wealthy merchant, Tunstall had been reared in a plush, fashionable London neighborhood. Now, the twenty-three-old adventurer stood within a sparse hamlet nestled in the Rio Bonito Valley, pressed between a slim meandering river to the north and steep mountains clad in timber to the south.[79]

Like other settlements in the territory, Lincoln consisted of a few dozen flat-roofed adobe homes and stores. Built with thick mud-brick walls to shut out the tiring heat of summer and the biting cold of winter, the buildings were scattered for nearly a mile on both sides of the town's only street, a hard-packed dirt road that could erupt in swirling dust one day and be deep in mud on another.

Tunstall spent his first two nights at Patrón's home and in the following days talked with several locals about life in Lincoln. "It's about the toughest little spot in America," Tunstall told his family in sharing the retelling of Ham Miller's murder of a local Mexican:

> A man can commit murder here with impunity. In talking of a man who had shot another here the other day for calling him a "gringo" (much the same as calling a Frenchman a "frog"), the [shooter] afterwards rode quietly up the town and told the sheriff 'he would like to see the man who could capture him'.

I said, 'He is rather bad medicine, I guess'. The man I was talking to replied, 'Who? Ham Mills? No! Not a bit of it! You never saw a better fellow than Ham anywhere. He gets mad quick and shoots quick, but he's a good shot and never cripples. None of his men [victims] have ever known what hurt them, and I really think he is sorry for it afterwards when he cools off'.[80]

Indeed, life in Lincoln was always lived at risk. The deadly combination of guns and whiskey could plant a man under a tombstone over the smallest argument or slightest perceived insult. In the eyes of some frontiersmen, it was less of a crime to kill a man than to steal his horse.

After enjoying a comfortable and restful first night at Patrón's place, Tunstall felt a twinge of remorse after being so critical of Patrón's driving on their grueling journey down from Santa Fe. "I really regret feeling so impatient with him on the road for his bad driving," he wrote, "for he is a very good fellow and considering [how limited] the chances he has had, I think him a wonder."[81]

On his second day in town, Tunstall introduced himself to Alexander McSween's wife, Susan. He found her to be very pleasant and was surprised she was the only white woman in town. She turned out to be very knowledgeable about Lincoln, providing Tunstall with the kind of information he was seeking. "She told me as much about the place as any man could have done," he marveled.[82]

Susan E. McSween

Built of stiffer emotional fiber than her husband, Sue McSween was restlessly ambitious and resolute in pursuit of wealth for herself and her husband. When she told Tunstall she had enemies in town, he assumed it was due to her husband's work as a lawyer. In truth, it was more about her incompatibility with Lincoln's predominant Hispanic population.

Like most Anglos, Sue viewed native residents as a lower class of people, and they resented her snobbery. Her dazzling gowns and elaborate makeup gave her an aura of superiority that did not set well with the native women, usually clad in simple dresses and blouses. Attracting attention whenever seen in town, Sue always was elegantly outfitted with her hair piled high in curls on top of a round, somewhat puffy face.

Tunstall liked what he learned from the McSweens and what he had seen for himself around Lincoln. Brushing aside his own assessment that life in Lincoln could be very dangerous, Tunstall decided he was going to settle in Lincoln and carve out his own modest empire with the goal of grabbing "one half of every dollar made by anyone in the county."[83]

Lincoln's residents soon took notice of the foreign aristocrat in their midst. His tall, slender frame, tucked neatly into a tailored riding outfit of fine broadcloth and high boots, drew stares from curious onlookers. He had a smooth face, topped by wavy, sand-colored hair, and sported a thin mustache and short chin whiskers, causing some to consider him handsome.

Tunstall's sharp British accent amused most listeners. To many of them, it exuded high education and wealth. He was the most unlikely newcomer to Lincoln, having inserted himself into the gritty tableau of frontier life: grubby farmers with long scruffy beards dragging in from nearby fields, saddle-sore cowboys whooping it up in noisy saloons after days on the range, and the mixed cacophony of children, dogs and chickens wandering everywhere.

Like other frontier towns, the center of life in Lincoln was its bustling plaza, pulsating with people coming and going. Black and white soldiers rode in from nearby Ft. Stanton, hungry for relief from military life. Locals gathered around, eagerly fetching the fresh fruits and buffalo jerky carried in on burros by the Pueblo and Apache Indians. Area farmers stood behind their stands, selling chickens, lambs and produce for the local cooking pots.

To the west of the plaza stood the Murphy-Dolan store, known by the local populace as the notorious "House." Around the two-story building was a scattering of adobe structures, including Sam Wortley's boardinghouse and several private homes, one of which contained a popular brothel. Between the House and the plaza stood a few more adobe homes, including the former Murphy branch store, now occupied by the McSweens as their temporary home.

Bordering the plaza was Jose Montano's store, the courthouse and the *torreon*, a tall adobe brick tower that sheltered the local citizens from marauding Indians whenever they went on a deadly rampage. Just east of the plaza was Patrón's twin-peaked adobe home and small mercantile store. Natives of lesser means lived in *jacals*, typical of the times. They were small homes crudely built of cedar posts, cinched together with mud plaster and covered by a dirt roof.

After McSween returned to Lincoln in December, he and Tunstall crafted a business plan to compete directly against the House, drawing upon McSween's privileged information about the House's business dealings, which he acquired while employed as the firm's lawyer. The two men made a formidable team. Tunstall had the zeal and money to take on the House, and McSween understood Lincoln's culture and knew the law. In the spring of 1877, they executed their plan by forming an unofficial partnership in the mercantile and banking businesses.

McSween's once amicable relationship with Murphy and Dolan had turned sour when he refused their demands that he defend a gang of cattle thieves caught red-handed stealing from herds owned by John S. Chisum, the largest cattle grower in the territory.

When Chisum heard about McSween's split with the House, he promptly retained the barrister to prosecute the thieves. In securing a conviction, McSween also established that the House's partner, John H. Riley, had colluded with the thieves to steal Chisum's cattle for a clandestine sale to the House. The case underscored Chisum's long-standing grievances with Murphy and Dolan. For years, his massive herds were thinned regularly by rustlers who found the House to be a ready buyer for their purloined beef at a lowly price of five dollars a head—with no questions asked. It was a cheap, easy way for the House to fill its government contracts.

When Tunstall and McSween established their Lincoln County Bank to undercut the House's high-interest lending practices, they hand-picked Chisum to serve as its president. This created a mighty trio against the House for economic dominance in the region. At any one time, Chisum maintained between sixty and eighty thousand head of high-grade Texas cattle on his Pecos ranges and employed more than a hundred cowboys and range workers to brand, herd and drive his animals to market.

For Tunstall and McSween, their principal business was in general merchandising, operating what would become known as the Tunstall Store. It was housed in a freshly built one-story structure adjacent to the plaza. The store stretched about one hundred feet along the town's main street and sat on the front edge of six acres McSween had acquired for one dollar from the Murphy-Dolan Company as settlement for legal fees owed to him. In the rear of the building, Tunstall lived in a small sparsely furnished apartment better suited for a Spartan.

On the back of the McSween property, the lawyer erected his unique nine-room dream home. It was U-shaped, overlooking the Rio Bonito, and lavishly furnished. Spectacular in its size, the home contained several bedrooms, a grand kitchen, McSween's law office and a spacious sitting room that housed a library and his wife's precious organ and piano. For a couple that arrived in Lincoln penniless, their extravagant spending caused some locals to wonder whether they came by their money honestly.

Once the Tunstall store began humming with steady customers, the Englishman turned his energies to fulfilling his most cherished dream, that of becoming a land baron with a huge stock-raising enterprise. With McSween's help, he filed a claim under the new Desert Lands Act for twenty-five-hundred acres in the lush, verdant Rio Feliz Valley, eighty miles southeast of Lincoln. The land lay on both sides of the slender river and reached nearly eight miles eastward from the Feliz's headwaters. With money sent to him by his father, Tunstall paid one thousand dollars for the land.

Additional money sent by his father enabled Tunstall to begin stocking his new range with cattle and a bevy of horses and mules for use by his range workers—all in preparation to compete with the House for government contracts to supply beef to Fort Stanton and the nearby Indian reservation.

Before Tunstall came onto the scene, the Murphy-Dolan company enjoyed a monopoly in just about every moneymaking venture in the county, be it by skullduggery in compromising besotted army officers to secure business favors or by controlling the county's legal machinery with its hand-picked officeholders. For years, the people of Lincoln County had depended solely on The House for their necessities of life. "Only those who have experienced it can realize the extent to which Murphy and Co. dominated the country and controlled the people, economy and politics," wrote Lily Klasner in her memoir. "To oppose them was to court disaster."[84]

In their pursuit of profits, Tunstall, McSween and Chisum had put their lives at risk by challenging the House, and eventually it would cost

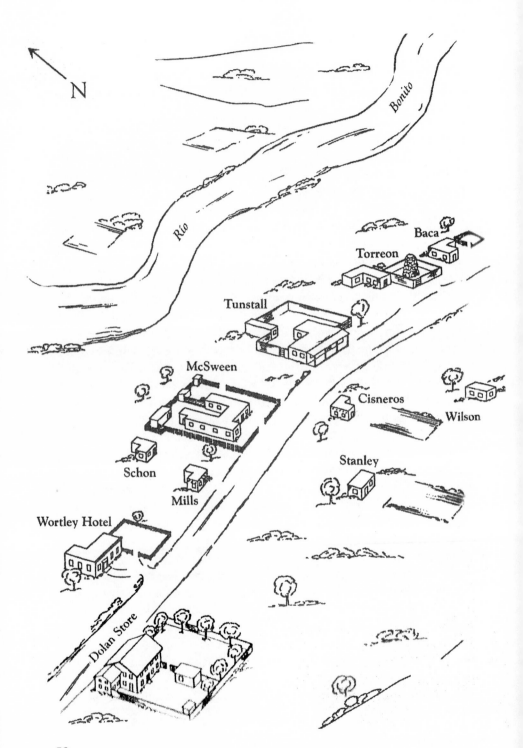

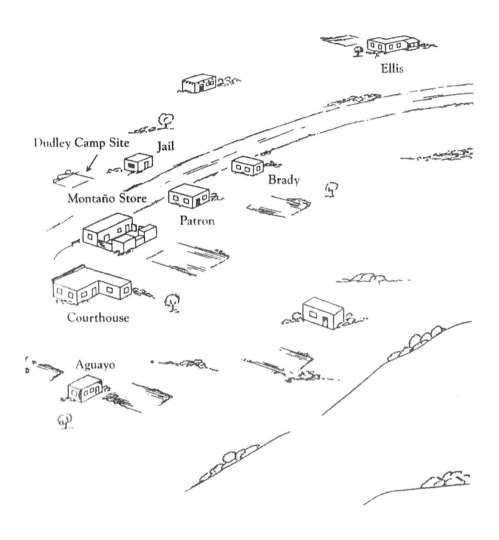

Ellis

Dudley Camp Site   Jail

Montaño Store

Brady

Patron

Courthouse

Aguayo

Lincoln when John Tunstall arrived in town

As reconstructed by Robert N. Mullin, Mullin Collection, Haley History Center, Midland, Texas. Adapted from the original in the Haley History Center.

two of them their lives. At this juncture, Juan Patrón could well have forecast the winds of war heading toward Lincoln, recounting later: "Mr. Tunstall came to this county, opened a store and by his straightforward course made friends with the people who preferred to trade with him rather than with Murphy, Dolan and Riley. This caused the enmity of them against Tunstall."[85]

Tunstall's plan to challenge the House was perfectly timed. Big changes were occurring in the House. In March, 1877, Murphy had become so consumed with drink, he was an alcoholic wreck. He withdrew from the business, passing it to Dolan and Riley to operate under the banner of the James J. Dolan Company. But the two remaining partners were left at the helm of a sinking ship. Rustlers wanted higher prices for their stolen cattle, and trading with farmers and ranchers produced no hard cash. The House was losing money fast.

CHAPTER 9

Mister Speaker

————◈◈◆◈◈————

As the Tunstall-McSween combine hammered away at Dolan's collapsing enterprises throughout 1877, Patrón was busy at the reins of local government as chairman of the county commissioners. He managed the levers of government much more deftly than his haphazard reining of the buggy team that carried him and Tunstall into town a few months earlier.

Patrón's first priority was to oversee the construction of Lincoln's first jailhouse, consisting of two underground cells built ten feet beneath the floor of a small house for the jailer. Eleven days after the jail opened on October 6, four of the county's most feared desperados—all Dolan henchmen—were hustled down the ladder into the dungeon-like cells. They were Jesse Evans and his sidekicks, namely Frank Baker, Tom Hill and George Davis, among their various aliases. Catarino Romero, a local thief, was put into one of the cells with them.[86]

Evans and his boys had been rounded up a day earlier by a posse led by Sheriff William Brady, after they stole two mules and several prized horses owned by Tunstall, who placed their value at seven hundred dollars. Now, the frontier thugs sat in irons in a dank jail pit that Pat Garrett later condemned as "unfit for a dog kennel." Boasting that their gang would bust them out, the boys passed their time playing cards, certain a plan was in preparation for their breakout.[87]

On November 7, Patrón received a note from Catarino Romero, who had escaped from the jail during an unforgivable lapse of judgment by the new jailer, Anselmo Pacheco. In his note, Romero revealed that Evans and his boys had filed through their shackles and augured holes in the jail's log walls with tools smuggled to them from the Dolan store.

Patrón notified Brady, and the two went together to the jail to see if Evans and his fellow thugs were free from their leg irons. Indeed, their shackles were severed. Maximiano de Guevara, the temporary jailer, begged that the prisoners be restrained with new shackles, but Brady brushed him off with a shrug of his shoulders. The next day, Patrón and his fellow commissioners appointed a new jailer, Diego Archuleta, to whom Brady was to give the jail keys but conveniently forgot to do so.[88]

During the dark hours of November 17, twenty horsemen from Evans's gang, including William H. Bonney (a.k.a. Billy the Kid), stormed the county jail. Half of them dismounted and pushed through the unlocked door of the jailer's house. Jailer Archuleta was sound asleep and shaken awake, staring wide-eyed at a gun barrel pressed against his forehead.

William H. Bonney, a.k.a. Billy the Kid

Archuleta sat helplessly as the invaders, using sacks filled with heavy rocks, battered the floor door leading to the dark cells below. When they busted through the door, they saw Jesse Evans and the other three gang members standing free from their shackles, waiting to climb the ladder to freedom.

The next morning, an angry Juan Patrón, joined by Tunstall and McSween, marched uptown to the Murphy store, where Brady made his headquarters, and confronted the sheriff. They insisted he raise a posse to go after the escapees and offered him twenty men. Brady, who owed his badge to Dolan, scoffed at the idea and snapped, "I arrested them once, and I'm damned if I am going to do it again. Hereafter, I am going to look after Brady's interest."[89]

A month later, Billy took his own turn inside Lincoln's hellhole after he was caught at Seven Rivers with a pair of horses belonging to Tunstall. Stewing in the jail pit did not sit well with Billy's freewheeling nature. At some point, he requested a meeting with Tunstall, and the two met. Their talk obviously went well because Tunstall arranged for the Kid's release and, in a surprise move, hired him to work at his Rio Feliz ranch.

It's not known what Billy promised in exchange for his release, but he was not above trading friendships for his freedom. In drafting her memoir, Lily Klasner believed that Tunstall only "pretended" to befriend the Kid so he could use him as "a tool" to testify against Evans for stealing the Englishman's horses and mules. "Billy was smart enough and coward enough to change crowdes [sic]," she wrote.[90]

Billy's friendship with Jesse had hit the rocks shortly after he joined the Evans gang, when he ran off with a favorite little racing mare belonging to the daughter of Mariano Barela, the county sheriff in Las Cruces. Billy didn't know that the lawman and Jesse were tight friends. Evans demanded that the Kid retrieve the mare for Barela after Billy had traded it for another ride. According to Lily Klasner, the mare ended up being purchased legally by her mother, who steadfastly refused Billy's pleadings to give up the spirited little horse. Tough as cedar bark, this frontier woman was not about to cave in to the thieving likes of Billy the Kid or Jesse Evans.[91]

The task of building Lincoln's notorious jail, unflatteringly described once by Pat Garrett as unable "to hold a cripple," had been left mostly to Patrón and Romero y Lueras. Their fellow commissioner Will Dowlin had been absent from their meetings since early summer when tragedy struck his family. On May 5, Will's brother, Paul, was murdered by one of their employees, Jerry Dillon, for no apparent reason.

The Dowlin brothers were well known in the county, operating a successful mercantile business and gristmill at Fort Stanton, where Paul served as the army post commander for a brief time as a Captain. Paul also had preceded Patrón as chairman of the county commission and when murdered was serving as a member of the Territorial House representing Lincoln, Grant and Doña Ana counties.

What is one man's loss often is another man's gain. When a special election was announced to fill Paul Dowlin's unexpired legislative term, Patrón decided to run for the seat. It would be his second attempt to represent Lincoln, Doña Ana and Grant counties in the house, having lost to John P. Risque in 1875. Heartened at being the first runner-up out of a field of five candidates in that race, Patrón was eager to try again.

Patrón quickly energized fellow Republicans in all three counties to rally around his candidacy. He had distinguished himself within the party the previous year when Lincoln County Republicans chose him to represent them at the party's state convention in Santa Fe. Clearly, Patrón had grown into a seasoned politician. He was well liked by fellow Mexicans and Anglos alike, and both viewed him as an honest and capable person who mixed easily within the two diverse cultures.

Lincoln citizens of all stripes fell in behind Patrón's candidacy, including arch enemies James Dolan and Alexander McSween. Both obviously wanted seats onboard Patrón's political bandwagon. They joined in publishing a petition to residents of Doña Ana and Grant Counties, asking them to support Patrón and assuring them of "his honesty, zeal and capacity."

Given that Doña Ana and Grant Counties were more thickly populated than their own county, the twenty-five petitioners said that special legislation was needed "to secure for us protection of life and property [and] to accomplish this, it is important that one of our citizens should be elected to present our views."[92]

Patrón's energetic campaigning paid off on November 10. He swamped his two opponents in a landslide victory, receiving five hundred and twenty-nine votes out of a total of six hundred and fifty-two votes cast in the three counties. Florencio Gonzales received eighty votes and H. W. Elliott, a dismal thirty-three votes. Patrón's victory came ten days before his twenty-fifth birthday, making him one of the youngest members elected to the territorial house.[93]

In Santa Fe, he would join forty-six-year-old John K. Houston of Grant County, elected previously to represent the same three counties as Patrón. Their counterpart in the Council, the upper body of the Legislative Assembly, was forty-four-year-old John S. Crouch of Mesilla.[94]

Soon after New Year's Day in 1878, Patrón set off on his four-day buggy ride to Santa Fe, a journey he had made many times before, usually seeking the governor's help to restore peace in Lincoln. On those trips, he was fraught with worry over his own safety and that of his family. On this trip, however, he felt happy at looking forward to being seated as a newly minted legislator. When Patrón arrived in Santa Fe, it was the weekend before the 23rd Legislative Assembly was to begin on Monday, January 7.

Like other legislators, Patrón settled into a local boardinghouse. There and around the capitol, he began mixing with other house members in small, informal gatherings, much like mini caucuses normally held by political parties to discuss legislative issues or choose leaders. For most of the men, these mixers were to socialize, get to know each other and, of course, talk politics.

Juan Patrón as young legislator

If the members-elect did split into political party caucuses, there is no record of doing so. By whatever method the newly elected house members had assembled formally or informally during that weekend, it would become apparent on Monday that Patrón had left last good impressions on those who had met him.

On Monday's opening day of the legislative assembly, Patrón rose early. He groomed himself carefully, shaving tightly around his thin mustache. Wearing a freshly ironed white shirt, he knotted a string tie into a neat bow, letting the ends dangle several inches in a somewhat dapper fashion. Then he slipped his arms into his favorite Prince Albert coat and hunched it onto his broad shoulders, completing his usual natty attire.

Stepping outside the boarding house on San Francisco Street, he felt the freezing air that overcast morning. Days before, it had been unusually warm for January. Now, swirling snow fueled by gusts of wind dusted the capital city's frozen dirt streets.[95]

Patrón limped his way toward a one-story, burnt-brown adobe structure that fronted on the town's main plaza. Known as the Palace of Governors, it housed the governor's living quarters and office and the legislative chambers of the house and council. Built in 1610, New Mexico's seat of government was one of the oldest public buildings in America. A block and a half away stood the lofty St. Francis Catholic Church, where Patrón had been baptized and received his first Holy Communion. The young legislator entered the church and knelt in thankful prayer, preparing to face one of the most momentous days of his life.

At high noon, Patrón and eleven other members-elect took their seats in Representative Hall and prepared to organize as an official and permanent body. However, they represented exactly half of the elected members to the house. Drifting snows across the territory prevented the other twelve members from reaching Santa Fe in time for the opening session.

Nonetheless, the assembled twelve members constituted a legislative quorum and as such proceeded to organize. Jose de Jesus Garcia of Socorro County, a veteran in his second term and one of the older members at forty-seven, was elected chairman pro tempore and gaveled the group to order. Then each member presented his credentials of election to a committee consisting of Perfecto Esquibel of Rio Arriba County, Jose Baca y Sedillo of Socorro County and John K. Houston, Patrón's cohort from Lincoln County. The three-man committee retired to a room outside the hall, reviewed the credentials and after a brief time reported to the body that all the credentials were accepted. At that point, all the members were "legally entitled to seats as members of the House."

In rapid succession, Rep. Perfecto Esquibel offered two motions, both adopted by voice vote. The first directed the body to proceed into a permanent organization of the House of Representatives. His second motion nominated Juan B. Patrón to serve as Speaker of the House. Whatever speeches were made on Patrón's behalf and his own words of acceptance are lost to history; the handwritten minutes of the house's legislative sessions during the 23rd Legislative Assembly are absent of any speeches.[96]

CHAPTER 10

Mr. Speaker and the Iron Horse

⸺◈⸱◈⸱◈⸺

A s Patrón led his house members through various parliamentary maneuverings during that first day as speaker, Tranquilino Labadie, his old high school buddy, sat in the public gallery, beaming with pride. Over the years, Tranquilino, now twenty-four, had become Patrón's closest advisor and confidant. It would be only three days hence that Labadie himself would be called into the great hall to serve as an officer of the house.

On January 10, the house received a communication from the secretary of the territory, nominating Labadie to serve as Interpreter of the House of Representatives during its current session. Representative Alejandro Branch of Mora County promptly offered a motion to approve the appointment, and when Speaker Patrón called for the yeas and nays, the motion carried 13 to 8 in favor. Now it was Patrón's heart that swelled with pride over his best friend's confirmation. After Labadie signed the Territorial Record, Patrón asked Secretary Ritch to swear Labadie into office.[97]

Like himself, most of Patrón's colleagues in the house were Hispanic. Of the twenty-four members who comprised the house, only four were Anglos. Despite the ethnic divide, the record indicates that the legislative members worked harmoniously throughout, without any visible conflict between the two cultures. Indeed, the bicameral assembly proved to be highly productive in a short period of time.

During its short life of six weeks, the 23rd Assembly passed thirty-four new general laws, ten acts specifically for local governments, one joint resolution, and eight "memorials" reflecting the assembly's position on certain issues. The legislators' workload that year proved historical in several ways for the young territory.[98]

Foremost, the Assembly passed three pieces of landmark legislation to enable the incorporation of railroad companies within the territory, leading to the opening of the New Mexico Division of the Atchison, Topeka and Santa Fe Railroad in Santa Fe on February 16, 1880. When enacted into law, these three measures alone resulted in thirty-eight pages of legal provisions, regulating what emerging railroad companies could or could not do.[99]

Besides setting the guidelines for the required articles of incorporation and corporate by-laws, the legislature established some rules peculiar to the territory's frontier character. It required that a corporation must have no fewer than five and no more than eleven directors, each owning at least ten percent of the corporate shares. All directors had to be American citizens and at least one-fourth of them had to reside within the territory. And all were to be elected for only one-year terms.

In a gesture toward equal rights among men and women, Patrón and his fellow legislators wrote into the railroad legislation that corporate shares owned by a married woman may be transferred or sold by her or her agent without her husband's signature, "as if such woman were a *feme sole*." Likewise, all dividends paid for shares held by a married woman would be paid to her as if she were unmarried.[100]

The legislature even went so far as to establish the maximum train fares allowed for carrying passengers and freight. For passenger trains, it would be unlawful to charge more than ten cents per mile for each passenger. No more than fifteen cents per mile could be charged for each ton of 2,000 pounds, or forty cubic feet of freight transported on a company's rails. The legislature also assured the railroads that in no case were they to receive less than twenty-five cents for any one lot of freight for any distance.

The new laws also gave the railroad companies the right to refuse to carry certain types of hazardous freight aboard their trains unless it was under specific conditions and freight rates established by the carrier. The restricted freights included domestic animals, nitroglycerin compounds, gunpowder, acids, phosphorus and other explosive or combustible materials.

For the "comfort and good behavior" of its passengers, railroad companies were forbidden to allow "gambling of every kind" on its cars, in its depots or on any station grounds. Rowdy and disorderly passengers could be expelled from the train by a conductor at the point of their misconduct. Railroads also had the right to refuse to carry "a person afflicted with any contagious disease or otherwise unfit to be admitted into its cars."[101]

Under the law, conductors also had to toe the line in their own behavior while working aboard a train. For example, if a conductor was found to be intoxicated while on the job, he faced a hefty fine of up to one thousand dollars or a six-month stay in the county jail, powerful incentives for any conductor to stay sober during his run.

For passenger safety, railroad companies also were forbidden to mix passenger cars with high value mail and freight cars or face a fine of $500. These non-passenger cars were seen by lawmen as lucrative targets for train-robbing desperados.

There were two other safety requirements. Each locomotive had to have a bell weighing at least twenty pounds attached to it, and the bell had to be rung no less than "eighty rods," or four hundred feet from the crossing of any public street, road or highway. The penalty for not doing so was a fine of one hundred dollars, half of which went to the territory and the other half to the violation whistle-blower. The railroad also was liable for all damages resulting from non-compliance.

The fact that the legislature deemed it imperative to write into law such rules of human behavior and protections against possible train robbers is indicative of the Wild West that prevailed in the New Mexico Territory at the time.

Not all of the provisions in these new railroad laws were restrictive and directing. Tax-wise, some were generous as well. To encourage construction of rail lines across the vast New Mexico Territory, "all property of every kind" owned by the railroad company newly incorporated in the territory was exempt "from taxes of every kind" for six years after completion of the new rail line—a government largesse that offered railroads a huge incentive to bring the "iron horse" into this frontier land. Towns and counties also were encouraged under the new laws to donate streets and highways to the railroads for access to their depots or stations within the donating towns and counties.[102]

Patrón, like his mentor Archbishop Lamy, believed that the surest cure for their territory's sickly economy was to be linked to the transcontinental railroad, being laid down at a rate of one mile a day. Both understood that the territory's agrarian economy, consisting mostly of raising sheep, cattle and a few crops, was inadequate to support a growing population when lands rich in minerals were waiting to be mined in the New Mexico Territory.

Ever the visionary, Lamy expressed it best: "When the rails are ready, the working of the mines, the raising of the flocks, the cultivation of the vineyards, will change entirely the conditions of things. We will be able to employ laborers at more reasonable wages, construct houses and churches as in the East. We may probably see factories established in this country, where wool is to be obtained in great abundance."[103]

To their dismay, Archbishop Lamy and the politicians in Santa Fe discovered the transcontinental rail line was going to bypass Santa Fe by some eighteen miles to the south and run directly to Albuquerque. These unhappy denizens of Santa Fe were determined to be connected to the railroad line, even if they had to pay for it themselves. Lamy successfully led a local effort to float a $150,000 bond issue to pay for a branch line from Galisteo Junction, later renamed Lamy, to Santa Fe.[104]

The first train to ride the branch line pulled in to Santa Fe on February 9, 1880, bringing to an end the days of the Santa Fe Trail. It marked the official completion of the Atchison, Topeka and Santa Fe line in New Mexico, just two years after Speaker Patrón and his house colleagues passed the enabling railroad laws. Patrón, along with Governor Lew Wallace, Chief Justice L. Bradford Prince and Army General Edward Hatch, were among the dignitaries celebrating the historic event.[105]

The coming of the railroads opened a new period of prosperity for the people of New Mexico. Rails laid for the new iron horse now linked the people in the industrial centers of the East with the farmers and miners living on the western frontier. Trains not only provided transportation for people but also carried products manufactured in the East to towns and cities in the West. And trains offered a faster way to ship cattle, sheep and wool from New Mexico to markets in the East and California.

The railroads changed New Mexico forever by eliminating its isolation and many of the hardships of frontier life. By 1885, nearly 1,300 miles of track had been laid down in the territory. Trains brought in tools and machinery for farmers and ranchers, helping them to boost their production, while the same trains carried the fruits of their labor back to hungry markets in the East and in California. In the northern reaches of New Mexico, the mines were booming because critical mining equipment made in the East was being shipped to them faster and more economically by rail. In the southeastern part of the territory, trains constantly brought new settlers to homestead the land and create new towns.[106]

The coming of the railroads also proved a boon to both schools and churches. Some locals jokingly referred to the combination as a "shotgun wedding" of churches, schools and the railroad. Where a school was built, a church followed; where a church opened, a school followed. Be whatever the combination was called, the schools and churches together formed the core of the new small towns that sprouted up like sunflowers along the railroad lines crisscrossing New Mexico in the 1880s.[107]

The railroad era brought new people to find work and settle in the young territory. New mines in the north and south opened, creating jobs mining silver, lead, zinc and coal. Lumbering, an industry new to New Mexico, began wherever timber was found in the mountains of the north and new farming lands were developed in valleys irrigated by the Pecos River.

These newcomers caused a major increase in the population of the territory. Totaling 119,565 in 1880, the population exploded to 160,282 by 1890. By then, three major railroads were operating at full-tilt in New Mexico, the territory's economy was booming and Speaker Patrón and his legislature had laid the groundwork to connect their homeland to the rest of the nation.

CHAPTER 11

Patrón and the Jesuits

———— ◆●◆◆◆◆ ————

J uan Patrón never suppressed his praise for the Christian Brothers who nurtured his intellect as a youth and molded him into an accomplished scholar at St. Michael's College. As one of the most knowledgeable men in New Mexico, Patrón put a high value on his education. Without the benefit of his studies in those first schools started by Bishop Lamy, he could never have become speaker of the house.

In the 1870s, New Mexico possessed only the rudiments of a public education system. One survey in 1872 showed that the territory had just forty-four primary schools, of which only five were public classrooms. Nearly all of the others were operated by the Catholic Church. The church's influence was so dominant in the territory that local politicians referred to the region as a "Catholic land" inhabited by a "Catholic people."[108]

Most boys' schools in New Mexico were operated by the Christian Brothers recruited by Bishop Lamy from his native France. Catholic girls' schools were run by either the Sisters of Charity or the Sisters of Loretto. The latter order was guided by the bishop's beloved niece Sister Mary Lamy, who as its popular leader was known as Mother Francesca.

Once centered only in Santa Fe, Lamy's schools slowly spread across New Mexico, and by 1878 eager young minds were filling new classrooms in Taos, Albuquerque, Los Alamos and Socorro, all built to meet the demand of an influx of immigrants from the East. Even with this growth, the young territory's educational base was sparse at best.

As a 25-year-old freshman legislator and newly minted speaker, Patrón's skills in parliamentary combat were yet to be tested. That soon changed. Just four days into the start of the 23rd Assembly, a dispute erupted over the question of providing tax relief for Catholic schools to be established by the Jesuits. The controversy rested in a measure passed earlier by the council senate and now sitting on the speaker's desk, awaiting consideration by Patrón and his house colleagues.

The council bill proposed the chartering of a small group of Jesuit priests to be known as "The Association of Jesuit Fathers of New Mexico." Typical of any corporation chartered by the territory, it could sue or be sued in local and state courts, and it could possess and dispose of real and personal property for the benefit and advancement of the society.[109]

The corporation's goal was "the education and development of the youth in all branches of letters, arts, and sciences" by establishing schools, colleges and other institutions as it deemed necessary in the New Mexico Territory. The corporation also was empowered to grant diplomas, confer degrees and other literary honors usually reserved for colleges and universities in the nation's public sector.

However, all of its properties, including real estate, would be exempt from taxes—a provision hotly contested by non-Catholic legislators and more so by top governing officers, including the governor and secretary of the territory. As expected, Bishop Lamy and the Jesuits were pressing hard for adoption of the tax waiver.

Lamy had been trying to recruit a Jesuit presence in his diocese since 1854, primarily to establish a small seminary for the education of young New Mexico men wishing to enter the priesthood. After two failed recruiting attempts over the next dozen years, Lamy finally met with success.

While in Rome in May 1867, Lamy made his third plea for Jesuits to be assigned to his diocese and won the support of Cardinal Alessandro Barnabo in the Vatican administration. At Barnabo's suggestion, Lamy put his request in writing, and Barnabo forwarded it to the current general of the Jesuits, Father Peter Beckx. When Lamy met with Beckx a few days later, the Jesuit leader assigned three priests and two brothers from Naples to the Santa Fe Diocese.[110]

Now, ten years later, five Jesuits were asking the legislature for tax relief to help them elevate the level of Catholic education in New Mexico. It was the Jesuits' first major push to establish institutions of higher education in the territory.

Those Jesuits identified as founders of the proposed corporation were Fathers Donato Gasparri, Rafael Baldosare, Luis Gentile, Salvador Persone and Pascuali Tomasine. All were pastors of parishes in the Counties of San

Miguel, Mora and Bernalillo. The notion that government should support the Jesuits' schools by exempting their taxes was met with resistance by opposing legislators and a sizable portion of the New Mexico press, setting off a legislative battle that would stretch from Santa Fe to the U.S. Capitol.

On Friday afternoon, January 11, 1878, one of the house's four veteran members, Perfecto Esquibel of Rio Arriba County, offered the perfunctory motion to remove the Jesuit bill from Speaker Patrón's desk. His motion carried, and the house began consideration of the measure, as it had been approved that morning by the council.

Immediately, two maneuvers were attempted that potentially could torpedo the bill. The first was a motion by Esquibel to refer the measure to a committee for further study. Uncertain of Esquibel's underlying motives, Patrón feared that such a move put the bill at risk of languishing in committee indefinitely. In a short but impassioned speech, Patrón challenged the motion and called for the vote. Esquibel's motion was defeated by a vote of seven to twelve.

Following that failed effort, Jose Baca y Sedillo, of Doña Ana County, offered an amendment to the bill that stated its intentions very clearly. It would require the Jesuit association to pay territorial taxes according to the laws of the land. After a vigorous debate, Patrón ordered a vote on the question, and the amendment failed by a vote of six to fifteen. It became apparent that the Jesuit bill was gaining support among house members.

Throughout the day, Father Gasparri, the superior of the Jesuits, worked furiously behind the scenes to prevent a repeated defeat of the same measure, rendered two years earlier by the previous legislative assembly. Conspicuous in his priestly white collar peeking out from under his long ecclesiastical garb, the cherubic-faced Jesuit leader dashed between the house and council chambers in the east wing of the Palace of the Governors, buttonholing legislators and urging them to support the tax relief bill.

Aware that most of the new members were Mexicans and Catholics, Gasparri immediately zeroed in on the political novices for support, especially Juan Patrón who held an enviable position of leadership and was well known as a Lamy loyalist. The forty-three-year-old Jesuit challenged the young legislators not to forsake their cultural origins. "You must be either Mexicans or gringos, and if you maintain yourselves, you must unite as Mexicans," the Jesuit reportedly told them. Gasparri's ethnically charged tactic may have garnered him votes, but it also brought him and his church severe rebukes in the widely read Santa Fe press.[111]

Reverend Father Donato Gasparri

By late afternoon, most house members became weary of listening to debate on the bill, and a call was made for final passage of the legislation, exactly as it was presented by the council. Speaker Patrón ordered the roll call. When the votes were counted, the measure carried fifteen to six, including a yes vote by Perfecto Esquibel, who earlier had tried to send the bill into committee. In the parliamentary tradition of the house, Speaker Patrón voted last, with a resounding aye.

Notwithstanding criticisms opined in the secular press, Father Gasparri proved to be an effective lobbyist. And the church's victory was trumpeted in the territory's most important Spanish-language newspaper, *Revista Catolica*, which Gasparri established almost singlehandedly in 1875 and remained its major contributing editor. By 1878, the weekly publication had more than one thousand subscribers, and Gasparri was becoming the best-known priest in all of New Mexico. Because his recall of knowledge was so enormous, he was nicknamed "The Walking Encyclopedia" by his admirers.[112]

Despite the ease with which the bill moved through the legislature, it ran into a political firestorm in Governor Samuel Axtell's office. This was not the first time Axtell, one of the rare Mormons in the region and an anti-Catholic Mason, was pitted against his old nemesis, The Reverend Donato Gasparri. They had battled over the tax relief question in the previous assembly. Although Axtell prevailed then, he still carried a belly full of disdain for the Jesuit, as evidenced in his veto message.

On January 18, Axtell returned the bill unsigned to both houses of the legislature with a blistering message, admonishing them for caving in to the wishes of the Jesuits. He declared their actions a violation of the laws of the United States.

Governor Samuel Beach Axtell in 1875

Casting aside Axtell's angry objections, the council approved the measure over the governor's veto by an eleven-to-two vote that afternoon. When the council's action was communicated to the house, Speaker Patrón began rounding up his members and reconvened the house at 3 p.m. to vote on the issue after reviewing Axtell's veto message. In opposing the bill, Axtell began by attacking its primary sponsor, Father Gasparri:

> It is difficult to decide whether the man who seeks to establish this society or the society which he seeks to establish is worse. Both are so bad you cannot decide between them. This Neapolitan adventurer, Gasparri, teaches publicly that his

dogmas and assertions are superior to the laws of the United States and the laws of the Territory. No doctrine or teaching can be more dangerous to good government than this, especially in New Mexico, where the masses of the people are ignorant. By his writings and harangues, he also endeavors to excite animosities and to stimulate the people to acts of violence towards those lawfully exercising civil authority over them.

Axtell found the bill especially objectionable on several fronts. It did not require the incorporators to be citizens of the United States nor residents of New Mexico. Nor did it limit the number of incorporators, including those who may reside abroad. It also empowered the Jesuits to own real and personal property free of taxation throughout the territory without any supervision by the legislature.

Attached to the governor's veto was a legal opinion he requested from Attorney General William Breeden, providing Axtell the legal basis for objecting to the proposed private charter of the Jesuits. In his report, Breeden declared that the Jesuit bill violated Section 1889 of the revised statutes of the United States, which read:

> The Legislative Assembly of the several territories shall *not* grant private charter of especial privileges, but they may by general incorporative acts permit persons to associate themselves together as bodies corporate for mining, manufacturing, or other industrial pursuits, or the construction or operation of railroads, wagon roads, irrigation ditches, and the colonization or improvement of lands in connection therewith, or for colleges, seminaries, churches, libraries, or any benevolent charitable, or scientific association.

By this section, Breeden explained that the Legislative Assembly of the Territory is "clearly prohibited from...creating any private corporation or granting it any special privileges," such as exempting property from taxation and granting powers to award diplomas and confer degrees—the two most important provisions sought in the Jesuit bill.

In the attorney general's opinion, the bill contained provisions Breeden considered to be "obnoxious to the prohibiting clauses of the law, no matter how meritorious the purposes of the proposed corporation may be." He warned that if the assembly insisted on adopting the measure over the governor's veto, it "would be invalid and of no effect."

Breeden concluded that unless the Jesuits wanted to form a corporation, liable for taxes, under the general incorporation act of New Mexico, they could not be incorporated in any other way. That said, the vote on Axtell's veto was drawing near.

Peering over his reading spectacles, Patrón carefully surveyed the number of members milling about in the house chamber. He saw that several members were absent. He needed to be certain that all the members were present to insure the required two-thirds vote to override the veto. Patrón then called for a count of members in the hall. Reps. Perfecto Esquibel, Wilson L. South and Jose M. Sanches were missing from the chamber. Their absence could make the override vote too close for Patrón's liking.

Drawing on a seldom-used parliamentary tactic, Patrón sought a call for *all* members of the house, which Rep. Branch readily provided him, and the doors were locked to keep members already in the chamber from wandering off. The speaker then ordered the sergeant at arms to "arrest" the three absentees and bring them before the bar of the house. Patrón was quickly learning the power of parliamentary protocols.

After a short absence, Sergeant at Arms Julian Baca returned to the house hall with Representatives Esquibel and Sanches in tow. Both members presented "satisfactory excuses" for their absences and were permitted to take their seats. Representative South had become ill and was excused by Patrón.

With his troops now corralled in the house, Patrón was ready to proceed. He gave a nodding cue to Rep. Branch, who obliged him with a call for passage of the Jesuit bill over the governor's objections. Patrón ordered the vote to be recorded. At the end of the roll call, eighteen yeas dominated the four nays. Patrón's tactic to search for Esquibel and Sanches rewarded him with an even larger margin of victory than when the bill originally passed the house by a fifteen-to-six vote.

While Patrón and his colleagues were basking in the glow of their victory over the governor, they were being hammered in the New Mexico press for "bending on knees" to the wishes of Father Gasparri. Several days later, the Grant County *Herald* weighed in editorially: "It is to the lasting disgrace of Juan B. Patrón of Lincoln County that he misrepresented his constituency by siding with and, in his feeble way, even attempting to lead the narrow-minded majority. The people of Grant, Doña Ana and Lincoln [counties] will probably bear Mr. Patrón well in mind, should he ever again aspire to office."[113]

Patrón probably shrugged off the *Herald's* chiding criticism. He had won election to the house by overwhelming majorities in Lincoln and Doña Ana Counties and even carried Grant County with its small voter turnout. Indeed, his support of the Jesuit bill may well have improved his standing with the voters at home.

Nevertheless, a serious movement to wrest control of New Mexico's school system from the Catholic Church by expanding free public schools was spreading across the territory. By the end of 1878, twelve of the fourteen newspapers in New Mexico, regardless of their political persuasion, had joined the crusade for public schools. Their entry into the fray triggered a heated exchange of editorials between the Catholic press and the non-sectarian press over the issue.[114]

The controversy stemmed from a conflict over basic philosophies. The Italian Jesuits who came to New Mexico found it difficult to adapt to a nation that separated church and state. The American concept of free public education was inconceivable to the Jesuits. They believed that church schools, based on the European model, served a higher purpose. Their beliefs were reflected in editorials in *Revista Catolica,* denouncing the nation's public school system and accusing it of producing "men without God and without religion, who have ruined the nation, and are dragging it down into the abyss of corruption." A radical denouncement, indeed![115]

The opposing secular press was equally radical in its treatment of the question and aroused the vicar-general of the Catholic diocese to respond with an official notice to the New Mexico newspapers. In it, he defended the teaching of sectarian dogmas at public expense, maintained that the American public school system "was the pampered child of impiety" and said the Jesuit fathers had been made "the target of a venal and shameless press."[116]

Months after Patrón and his fellow legislators adjourned and returned home, Secretary of the Territory W. G. Ritch began work on a plan to override the new act chartering the Jesuit fathers. Ritch was a seasoned warrior in the fight for free public schools. In 1875, he drafted a school bill that, for the first time, denied public funding of Catholic schools and declared public schools as critical to the modernization of New Mexico. Jesuit priests, again led by Father Gasparri, mounted a mighty effort to defeat the bill in the territorial legislature but failed.[117]

Ritch believed that the Jesuits' effort to submerge public schools in

New Mexico was the seed of a Roman-Catholic conspiracy to undermine public education in America. Sending this warning to U.S. Commissioner of Education John Eaton, Jr., Ritch asked that Congress take control of the situation. He urged that Congress annul the Jesuit charter because it violated section 1889 of the U.S. Revised Statutes, which prohibits the granting of private charters of especial privileges.

Congress obliged Ritch in February 1879. The house and senate unanimously adopted legislation that annulled the Jesuit charter, and President Hayes signed the measure into law. For Patrón and the Jesuits, it was a crushing defeat. The public school victory was exulted in the New Mexico press, perhaps at its height by the *Daily New Mexican*, which gloated in an editorial: "The patriotic citizens of every State and Territory may likewise take to themselves congratulations that Jesuits and Jesuitism at large has thus had a most severe and telling rebuke administered to them at the hands of the highest tribunal of forty-five million freemen." It was an unexpected setback for the Jesuits who essentially had laid the foundation of Catholicism in the English-speaking Colonies.[118]

Father Donato Gasparri was archetypical of what some in the priestly order call the "Jesuit brand"—an ethos of people who are highly educated and activists in causes they ardently try to propagate. Congress' undoing of his measure was a disappointing blow to Gasparri, but the Jesuit moved on to new challenges with undiminished fervor.

The Jesuit bill was one of five measures vetoed by Governor Axtell, all overridden by the assembly. Among them was another Catholic bill of much lesser note. It proposed financial support for San Vicente Hospital, operated by the Sisters of Charity in Santa Fe. The hospital's primary mission was to care for "the poor, sick and orphans, regardless of their race, position or religious belief." As passed, the bill provided a monthly appropriation of $100 to the hospital out of any territorial funds, not otherwise appropriated, for use by the hospital. An oversight council, consisting of the Archbishop of Santa Fe, the secretary of the territory and the hospital physician, also was established to oversee the hospital's expenditure of the monthly stipend.[119]

For a novice legislator propelled into the speakership at such a young age, Patrón maneuvered through a daunting legislative agenda with relative ease. Unfaltering throughout, he mastered parliamentary procedure and marshaled his colleagues to an emotional victory—albeit short lived—in one of the most divisive issues regarding education in New Mexico's early history.

CHAPTER 12

The Murder of John Henry Tunstall

By the time snow began gathering in Lincoln in 1878, the once powerful Murphy-Dolan enterprise was on its knees. Starved for cash, the crippled firm no longer could pay its rustlers for stolen cattle to fulfill its once lucrative government contracts. Farmers who once exchanged their crops for advanced credit now turned to Tunstall for bartering. The combined effect had the company teetering on the brink of bankruptcy.

James J. Dolan in 1879

In a desperate move to save the company, Dolan turned to Attorney General Thomas B. Catron, the Santa Fe ringmaster, for help. On January 12, 1878, the Dolan Company mortgaged everything to Catron—its store, land, merchandise, grain, hay, cattle and horses. If Dolan hoped to regain the upper hand in this struggle for economic dominance, he had to eliminate his competition in one way or another. He turned to the gun for a solution.

When John Tunstall decided to settle in Lincoln, no one foresaw that Juan Patrón had brought to town the man whose ambitions would ignite one of the most famous and bitter feuds in the American West, known as the Lincoln County War. It became a violent conflict for economic dominance, fueled by greed, the ubiquitous six-shooter and an endless flow of high-octane whiskey.

Before their war turned bloody, Tunstall and Dolan confined their attacks against each other to non-violent ways. Throughout 1877, each spewed vicious rumors about the other. Both publicly exchanged ugly accusations in the territorial press, and each had turned to litigious warfare in trying to bring down the other.

Both sides, however, prepared themselves for eventual violence, bringing onto their payroll men who knew how to handle a Colt six-shooter and a Winchester repeater. This probably was Tunstall's *real* reason for hiring Billy the Kid as a ranch hand. Those who had crossed Billy's path knew he was no true cowboy but could handle a six-shooter and carbine better than most.

Lily Klasner, who was no fan of Billy's, was impressed with his riding and shooting after he first rode into Lincoln County in 1877 and showed up at the homestead of her father, Robert Casey, looking for work. "He was as graceful as a cat...and practiced continually with a pistol or rifle, often riding at a run and dodging behind the side of his mount, as the Apaches did," she recalled. However, the Casey family judged him to be little more than a bum, who "was not addicted to regular work," and told the Kid to move on.[120]

After Billy was turned away at the Casey place, he drifted onto Frank Coe's ranch on the Rio Ruidoso, hoping for a job there. The Kid was still a scrawny teenager with barely more than peach fuzz sprouting on his chin. Coe thought the Kid was too young for the rigors of ranch work but invited him to stay until he could find work elsewhere.

Billy proved to be good entertainment for Coe and his ranch hands whenever he played with his shooting irons. "He spent all of his spare time cleaning his six-shooter and practicing shooting," Coe said. "He could take two six-shooters, loaded and cocked, one in each hand, his fore-finger between the trigger and guard, and twirl one in one direction and the other in the other direction, at the same time." This was high praise from a frontier-toughened man, who was plenty handy with a gun himself and could shoot one quickly.[121]

Tunstall's hiring of the Kid put a highly skilled gunslinger on his side as his war with Dolan was turning hotter. By February 1878, the legal sniping between McSween and Dolan reached fever pitch with criminal and civil suits crisscrossing almost daily in the district courts.

On February 7, Dolan finally achieved the upper hand in their litigious warfare. Through his cozy relationship with the district court in Le Mesilla, he finagled a writ to attach McSween's property as security in a freshly penned ten thousand dollar civil suit filed against the lawyer by two Dolan loyalists.

Dolan rushed the writ one hundred miles north to Lincoln, slapped it into the hands of Sheriff William Brady, his obedient lackey, and told him to carry out the court order post haste. That simple, routine court order would spawn the bloody tragedy soon to befall McSween and Tunstall.[122]

Like most people in Lincoln, Brady believed that McSween and Tunstall were formal partners, even though their alliance, in fact, was based on no more than a handshake to seal certain verbal promises. In Brady's eyes, however, what belonged to Tunstall also belonged to McSween and could be attached.

The next day, Brady and his posse stormed into McSween's home and office and impounded all of his possessions under the writ of attachment. They also took over the Tunstall store, closing it for business, and inventoried all of its merchandise. Then, Brady took the daring step of trying to attach each man's land, cattle and horses—their total value far exceeding the ten thousand dollars being secured under the writ.

When Tunstall returned two days later from St. Louis, he was outraged at Brady's actions. His natural aversion to violence was fast being overtaken by a mounting willingness to meet violence with violence, if that was Dolan's choosing. Ever since Jesse Evans and his boys ran off with Tunstall's horses the previous October, he began hiring ranch hands who knew the workings of a Winchester and Colt better than the handling of cattle.

Soon after Billy signed on at the Feliz ranch, Dick Brewer, a steady hand already on Tunstall's payroll, began assembling a formidable team of warriors for his boss. Each was promised a princely four dollars a day if sent into war. Brewer, known as a crack shooter, recruited John Middleton, a fearless drifter able to shoot fast and accurately, and Henry C. Brown and Fred Waite, both confirmed as skilled gunmen. Billy and Waite, a part-Chickasaw Indian who was six years older, soon became inseparable as Tunstall's bodyguards.

On February 11, an irate Tunstall and his trusty foreman, Robert Widenmann, charged into the Englishman's store and challenged Sheriff Brady and his inventory. With palms resting on the handles of their pistols, they demanded that Brady release from his inventory six horses and two mules that were corralled behind the store. To back up their demand, Bonney and Waite stood outside the doorway with their Winchesters at the ready. Brady relented without argument, and Tunstall told Widenmann to drive the animals back to the Feliz and that he would follow later.

Two days later, at Dolan's insistence, Brady sent his deputy, Jacob B. "Billy" Mathews, and a four-man posse, all Dolan employees, to impound all of the stock at Tunstall's ranch. As Mathews and his posse approached the ranch's two-room adobe, Brewer and Widenmann stepped outside with their Winchesters dangling at their sides. They warned they would not give up any of Tunstall's stock without a fight. When Mathews spotted Bonney, Waite and Middleton lurking in the shadows to back up the promise, the posse turned tail and galloped back to Lincoln for new instructions.

Foiled but undeterred, Dolan and Brady decided they needed a larger posse. While Mathews went looking for more men in Lincoln, Dolan reached into his cow camp on the Pecos and ordered William "Buck" Morton, his foreman, to find some Seven River stockmen to join the posse. Morton promptly recruited nine willing riders, including ranchers Bob Beckwith and Wallace Olinger, each dexterous in drawing and shooting a pistol.

On the night of February 17, the Mathews posse, bolstered by more fire power, was poised to charge the Tunstall ranch from its camp eight miles south of the Feliz. The posse had grown to twenty-three well-armed riders, including Dolan, plus three insistent tagalongs, Jesse Evans, Frank Baker and Tom Hill, who ostensibly wanted to recover a horse Evans had loaned to Billy Bonney.

In the meantime, Tunstall learned that the swollen posse intended to charge his ranch, seize his cattle by force and kill all of his ranch hands. Hearing this, Tunstall left Lincoln, raced back to the Feliz, and decided to give up his cattle rather than risk his men's lives in a shootout.

While the Mathews posse rested overnight at its nearby encampment before attacking the Feliz the morning of February 18, Tunstall and his five warriors saddled up at first light and started driving nine horses back to Lincoln to save them from impoundment. Six of the horses were the ones Brady had been forced to release one week earlier, and the other three belonged to Brewer and Bonney.

When Mathews and his men reached the Feliz that morning, one of the two ranch hands left behind, Godfrey Gauss, the cook, said his boss and horses had left at daybreak. Dolan was irate at being outmaneuvered and insisted that the horses had to be attached along with the cattle. Dolan and Mathews chose fourteen men as a sub-posse to chase after Tunstall. Again, Jesse Evans insisted that he and his boys ride along to retrieve the horse he loaned to Bonney.

Mathews deputized William "Buck" Morton to lead the smaller posse. Taking charge, Morton let it be known he had more on his mind than recovering horses as he shouted out, "Hurry up boys, my knife is sharp and I feel like scalping someone."[123]

By the time dusk was gathering, the Tunstall party had put thirty miles between themselves and the Feliz. While Tunstall, Brewer and Widenmann maneuvered the horses through the rugged hills, some three thousand feet above Lincoln, Bonney and Middleton protected the rear a few hundred yards behind. Waite had been sent to Lincoln with a buckboard on an easier path below the hills.

As Tunstall and his men crested a high divide and began riding single file down a steep, winding canyon leading to the Ruidoso Valley, they startled a flock of turkey that took wing. At Tunstall's behest, Brewer and Widenmann chased after the birds on a sporting hunt, leaving the Englishman alone with the horses.

Moments later, shots rang out at the rear of the trail. Bonney and John Middleton rushed forward at a gallop. Riding hard behind them were Mathews and his men, draped with cartridge belts.

While Middleton raced toward their boss, Bonney split off and joined Brewer and Widenmann, who upon hearing the gunfire took cover on a rocky hillside where they planned to make a stand behind some large boulders.

Middleton shouted at Tunstall to flee, but the Englishman, confused by the gunfire and commotion, did nothing. "For God's sake, follow me," Middleton pleaded one last time before dashing for cover.

"What, John? What do you say, John?" was all Tunstall managed to ask.[124]

When the posse saw Tunstall all alone, the pursuers rushed toward him. The first men to approach him were Buck Morton and Tom Hill. Tunstall knew they were Dolan's hired guns and froze. Hill told Tunstall if he surrendered he would not be hurt, so Tunstall slowly nudged his horse toward them. When he came closer, Morton, without warning, sent a rifle bullet into the Englishman's chest.

Tunstall tumbled out of his saddle and crashed to the ground. Hill then jumped from his horse, stood over the man and fired his pistol into the back of Tunstall's head. Crouched behind their cover on the hillside, Tunstall's men heard the shots but could not see what happened. But they knew Tunstall had been killed.

Ignoring the whereabouts of Bonney and the other Tunstall men, the posse placed the dead man's body on an open blanket, covering it with a second one. Then, one of the men placed the Englishman's overcoat under his bleeding head. Tunstall's horse, which Tom Hill had shot dead, was lying next to its owner. In a bizarre act, someone stuffed Tunstall's hat under the horse's head.

Rather than look for the rest of Tunstall's party, the posse rounded up the scattered horses and headed them back to the Feliz to join Dolan and Mathews. Bonney and the others waited for darkness before riding back to Lincoln, reaching town near midnight. They left Tunstall's body behind to be dealt with the next day.

As the tragedy of John Tunstall's killing was unfolding, Juan Patrón was busy in Santa Fe as Speaker of the Territorial House, guiding his legislative body through its final paces before adjourning *sine die* on February 15. When the Lincoln legislator returned home, he was shocked and saddened by his friend's violent death.

What Patrón didn't know was that he also was being targeted by the Dolan faction. District Attorney William Rynerson uncorked the plot in a letter to his "Friends Dolan and Riley" on February 14. "Get the people behind you," he told them. "Control Juan Patrón, if possible. You know how to do it. Have good men about to aid Brady and be assured I shall help you all I can."[125]

As undisputed leader of Lincoln's Hispanic population, Patrón influenced a majority of the townspeople. For their own safety, he had dissuaded them from taking up arms for either side in the war fomented by Dolan, even though he personally supported the McSween-Tunstall faction. Dolan followed a simpler code of allegiance: if you don't stand with me, then you stand against me.

On the night of February 19, Patrón joined a small clutch of townspeople standing on the side of Lincoln's main street as the slain John Henry Tunstall was brought into town in the back of a wagon and carried into his store. Tunstall's body was a bloody mess as two men placed it on a table.

The bullet that slammed into the back of Tunstall's head had plowed through his brain and exited above the left eye. His fine clothes were tattered and his face badly scratched from being draped over the back of a mule as it brushed past brambles and scrub oaks on its way down the mountains.

While two doctors performed an autopsy on Tunstall's body, Billy Bonney walked in, stared down at the corpse for a silent moment and hissed, "I'll get some of them before I die." Bonney had come to like his boss a great deal, even though he had known Tunstall less than three months. He later admitted to an acquaintance that Tunstall was the only man who treated him as if he were "freeborn and white."[126]

One of the two men who surveyed Tunstall's fatal wounds that day was Dr. Taylor F. Ealy, a newly arrived medical missionary from Pennsylvania. Ealy and his family had ridden into town atop their packed buckboard just hours before. They had come to Lincoln in response to McSween's request the previous autumn that the Presbyterian Church detail a minister to start a church in town.

The arrival of the Ealy family was fortuitous, indeed. Not only did Ealy assist in the autopsy and embalming of Tunstall's body, McSween asked the preacher to officiate at a funeral service for his slain friend. A grave was dug just east of the Tunstall store for the Englishman's burial.

On the afternoon of February 21, many of the townspeople gathered to hear Dr. Ealy's funeral oration and to pay their personal respects to the man who had freed them from Dolan's economic tyranny. Susan McSween's organ sat at the graveside, and because she was visiting family back East, the new preacher's wife, Mary Ealy, played several hymns while Juan Patrón led a few of the men in singing.[127]

Patrón's hardy baritone voice stood out among the singers, as they opened the ceremony with the hymn, "Jesus Lover of My Soul," sending forth the words, "You have taken me from the miry clay, set my feet upon the Rock and...though my world may fall, I'll never let you go...."

Dr. Ealy delivered his sermon, postulating that beyond this life, man "shall live again" and dwell in "Our Father's House." Surely, he told his listeners, the dead man's "dear parents" would one day be reunited with their departed son. As the preacher delivered his words, Justice John B.

Wilson translated for the Hispanics standing among the mournful.[128]

The Patrón choir closed the service with "My Faith Looks Up To Thee," ending with the doleful words, "When death's cold, sullen stream shall o'er me roll...O bear me safe above, a ransomed soul." McSween later wrote Tunstall's family that "not a dry eye was in the audience."[129]

As McSween's black servant, Serbian Bates, shoveled clumps of dirt onto Tunstall's coffin that day, the wily foe who engineered his death was galloping to Mesilla. Jimmy Dolan wanted a fresh warrant from his friend, Judge Bristol, for the arrest of McSween, still skirting jail and facing a criminal charge of embezzlement.

Dolan also had instructed his partner John Riley to enlist the military at Fort Stanton to help Sheriff Brady serve the warrant once it reached his hands, and if need be, he told Riley, alert Jesse Evans to be prepared "to do his part" once the soldiers departed. Those were ominous words. McSween knew he if he ended up in Lincoln's jail, he would be killed by Evans, so he decided to flee.

McSween did not go far. With Bonney, Waite and Brewer riding at his side, the lawyer and his trio of gunslingers took refuge in the hills outside of Lincoln and made battle plans. Although he never holstered a gun in his life, McSween reluctantly assumed the role of leader in the fight against the Dolan faction, even if it led to more bloodshed.

Although McSween technically was a fugitive by resisting being jailed, he insisted his group remain on the right side of the law and turned to Justice Wilson for help. Wilson was an honest but bumbling old man, barely literate and easily persuaded. But he had the power to issue arrest warrants, and his constable, Atanacio Martinez, could raise a lawful posse.

At McSween's behest, Wilson issued arrest warrants for eighteen members of the Mathews posse, including Dolan and Buck Morton. All were charged with the murder of John Tunstall. At the same time, Dick Brewer had Wilson appoint him as a special constable and began forming a posse from the forty men Tunstall recruited before his death in anticipation his feud with Dolan could turn bloody.

Brewer and his posse called themselves the Regulators. For once in his life, Billy Bonney found himself riding on the right side of the law. Well-armed with plenty of cartridges stuffed into their belts, the Regulators were ready for a fight.

While Tunstall's was the first blood spilled in the Lincoln County War, more bloodshed was on the horizon. On March 6, eleven Regulators, led by Brewer and including Bonney, spotted five of Dolan's hired gunmen near the junction of the Rio Penasco and the Pecos. When the Regulators gave chase, the five riders split up. Bonney recognized Buck Morton and Frank Baker and galloped after them. The other Regulators quickly joined him in the chase.

Brewer's men chased the pair for several miles, all the while emptying their six-shooters and carbines without landing a single shot. By then, Morton's and Baker's mounts were exhausted, and both stumbled in the rocky terrain, throwing horses and riders to the ground. Morton and Baker quickly scrambled for cover and prepared to make a fight of it. But Brewer, a gentle giant with massive arms and huge hands, talked them into surrendering with the promise they would be taken into Lincoln safely.

Brewer's promise infuriated Bonney. He wanted to avenge Tunstall's death by killing Morton on the spot. When he tried to rush Morton, several Regulators grabbed the feisty kid and physically restrained him as Bonney angrily hissed, "My day will come."[130]

On their way back to Lincoln, a former Tunstall employee, William McCloskey, joined the Regulators near Roswell. He was a friend of Morton's and boasted he was there to guarantee no harm would come to Morton or Baker. His mission didn't set well with some of the other Regulators, especially Frank McNab.

As the gang and prisoners maneuvered through the Agua Negra Canyon about twenty miles out of Roswell, McNab, a former "cattle detective" for cattle baron John Chisum, quietly rode up behind McCloskey. Without warning, he yanked out his pistol, aimed it at McCloskey's head and roared, "So you are the son of a bitch that's got to die before harm can come to these fellows, are you?"[131]

As his words melted in the air, McNab squeezed the trigger of his gun, and McCloskey tumbled from his saddle and fell dead to the ground. Seeing this, Morton and Baker knew what was in store for them. They buried their spurs deep into the bellies of their worn-out horses in a desperate attempt to get away.

The fleeing pair galloped only a few hundred yards in their escape before a roaring fusillade of gunfire from the Regulators blew them from their saddles. When their pursuers examined the dead men, Morton had been shot nine times, and Baker five.

Bonney's shooting irons were smoking hot and surely had delivered some of Morton's fatal wounds. The Regulators left the three bodies to bloat under the day's sun. Days later, they were buried in shallow graves by passing sheepherders.

"Of course, you know, I never meant to let those birds reach Lincoln alive," Bonney later admitted to his friend George Coe, obviously taking satisfaction in avenging Tunstall's murder.[132]

While the Regulators continued to pursue their brand of justice, Dolan and Riley turned to powerful allies in Santa Fe for help. Chiefly through Thomas B. Catron, who held the mortgage on their properties, and their friend Rynerson, they landed Governor Samuel B. Axtell in their camp.

On March 4, Axtell delivered the first of two mighty blows to McSween and the Regulators. He telegraphed President Rutherford B. Hayes, urging him to direct federal troops to help enforce civil order in Lincoln. Within days, the Fort Stanton garrison received orders to assist the territorial civil officers, namely Bristol, Rynerson and Brady, in upholding the law. The Army now stood on the side of the Dolan faction.

On March 9, the governor made a quick three-hour visit to Lincoln, supposedly to learn firsthand about events there. Already swayed by the Catron-Rynerson version of the conflict, Axtell had no time for anyone partial to McSween's cause, especially Juan Patrón. The governor was still smarting from Patrón's legislative whipping, overriding Axtell's veto of the measure to exclude the Jesuits of New Mexico from taxation.

In Lincoln, the governor delivered a second blow more devastating than the first. He issued a proclamation that voided John B. Wilson's appointment as justice of the peace by Patrón and his fellow county commissioners the previous year, thereby invalidating Brewer's commission as deputy constable and arrest warrants for Tunstall's murderers. Patrón's commission had chosen Wilson to fill the seat of Justice James Farmer after he resigned for personal reasons in February 1877.[133]

With the stroke of his pen, Axtell wrecked the legal apparatus McSween had assembled to empower the Regulators to execute arrest warrants within the law. Now, he and his Regulators were outlaws and faced arrest for the killing of Morton, Baker and McCloskey. To avoid arrest, Brewer and the rest of the Regulators fled into the mountains, while McSween and his wife Sue found safety at John Chisum's ranch on the Pecos, fifty miles east of Lincoln.

Near the end of March, the Regulators decided, with or without McSween's blessing, Sheriff Brady had to be eliminated to protect their leader from being killed when he came to Lincoln in April to face embezzlement charges before Judge Bristol. "Brady is going to try and arrest me, and you should not let him get away with it," McSween reportedly told a group of Regulators he met at Chisum's ranch. "If I am arrested, I shall surely be hung, and I don't want to die."[134]

On the night of March 31, an execution party of six Regulators quietly crept into the empty corral behind the Tunstall store. Shielded from Lincoln's main street by an adobe wall, the group consisted of Frank McNab, Billy Bonney, Fred Waite, John Middleton, Henry Brown and "Big Jim" French. Their target was Sheriff Brady.

Early on the morning of April 1, Brady sauntered into Wortley's Hotel for his usual breakfast. When he took the last swallow of his morning meal, the lawman brushed his massive mustache clean and headed out to his office in the Dolan store. There, the sheriff collected his four deputies— Billy Mathews, George Hindman, John Long and George Peppin.

Walking next to their five-feet-eight-inch, blue-eyed sheriff, the lawmen headed east for the courthouse to post a notice that district court would begin its spring term on April 8 and not this day as erroneously advertised. Stuffed in one of Brady's pockets was the arrest warrant for McSween in hopes the lawyer would come to Lincoln that morning for court. Serving it would give Brady great pleasure and his friends the upper hand in their feud with McSween.

As Brady and his deputies passed the wall shielding the men crouched behind it, the executioners reared up, leveled their carbines and unleashed a volley of crackling gunfire. Brady, pummeled repeatedly by lead slugs, staggered backwards and fell dead to the ground. A dozen bullets riddled his body. Hindman also took a round in the chest during the fusillade. As he lay moaning for water, a second rifle shot from behind the wall sent him into final darkness.

During the opening fire, Brady's other deputies scampered for cover wherever they could find it. Justice Wilson, an innocent bystander, was not so lucky. A wayward bullet pierced both of his thighs while he was hoeing onions at his home across the street. He dropped to his knees in agonizing pain.

Bonney and Jim French raced from the corral to Brady's body and bent down in search of the warrant for McSween's arrest. With the groping pair unshielded and in full view, Mathews and the other deputies opened fire. As bullets kicked up dust around them, Bonney and French made a frantic dash back to the corral. As they ran, a bullet drilled through the soft flesh of French's thigh. Both reached the corral safely but without the precious warrant or the sheriff's Winchester that Bonney had tried to grab. After hiding French from the surviving deputies, the Regulators mounted their horses and galloped out of town unmolested.[135]

Like his friends Jimmy Dolan and John Riley, the forty-eight-year-old Brady was a native of Ireland. Most of his fifteen years in the regular army had been spent fighting Indians. After a short stint with the New Mexico Volunteers, he settled in Lincoln and soon fell under the influence of the House. As Murphy's handpicked candidate, Brady first was elected county sheriff in 1869 and again in the 1876 elections when Patrón won his seat on the Lincoln County Commission.

Despite Governor Axtell's proclamation placing them outside the law, the Regulators believed they still were justified in hunting down the men who murdered Tunstall, and they didn't plan to stop. Three days after Brady's death, fourteen Regulators, led by Dick Brewer and including the wounded Jim French, stopped at Blazer's Mill, a small settlement founded by Dr. Joseph H. Blazer, the only dentist in the area. While eating lunch at the Blazer residence, they spotted Andrew "Buckshot" Roberts, a scrappy stockman who rode with the Mathews posse that killed Tunstall. Roberts's name was on the arrest warrant issued by Justice Wilson, which had become just a worthless piece of paper, though not to the Regulators.[136]

When they bounded out of the house intending to arrest Roberts, they were greeted with gunfire. The first Regulator hit was John Middleton. He took a slug in the lung. The next round from Roberts's carbine smashed into Charlie Bowdre's massive belt buckle, probably saving him from a fatal wound in the gut. Another shot mangled George Coe's right thumb and trigger finger, which he later lost to a surgeon's knife. Badly outnumbered, the fearless Roberts held his ground as he cranked the lever of his Winchester, delivering shots with remarkable accuracy.

When Bonney thought Roberts had emptied his Winchester, he crept to a safe spot where he had a shot at Roberts, now barricaded inside a doorway to Blazer's dental office. Bonney fired at the open doorway. It was not a clean shot but a lucky one. The slug passed through the thin doorframe, cut through Roberts's stomach and exited above the right hip. Refusing to give up, Roberts swallowed the pain and rearmed himself with an old .45-70 Springfield long-range hunting rifle and cartridges he found inside the office.

In the meantime, Brewer positioned himself about a hundred yards away for a straight shot at Roberts through the doorway. The first shot from his Winchester missed, and Roberts saw the smoke flume from Brewer's gun. When Brewer popped up for his second shot, Roberts fired. The bullet flew into Brewer's forehead and seared through his brain, and the twenty-eight-year-old blond, blue-eyed giant crashed to the ground like a fallen oak.

Brewer's death not only left the Regulators leaderless, it sent their morale into a tail spin. Disgusted and bloodied, they mounted their horses and rode off, leaving the Blazers to bury Brewer and to deal with Roberts. Bleeding and in great pain, Roberts died the next morning, and he and Brewer were buried on a hill overlooking the small settlement. Roberts's gallant stand against great odds won Frank Coe's admiration. He later said Andrew "Buckshot" Roberts probably was the bravest man he ever knew.[137]

Following the deaths of Brady and Roberts, public support for the Regulators evaporated quickly. Killing a county sheriff in an ambush was seen as cowardly and violated the code of fair play that most people expected. Roberts's death also was viewed as an unfair fight forced by the Regulators. To a growing number of people, Brewer's men were considered no better than Dolan's hired guns who rode in Brady's posse.

It was impossible for Patrón to lower his visibility in Lincoln. Despite gunfire crackling all around him and threats on his life, he remained above the fray. Besides, he had a county to govern as chairman of its commissioners. With Brady's death, Patrón's commission rushed to find a new, impartial sheriff. Ruling out all of Brady's partisan deputies for the job, the commission on April 10 appointed John A. Copeland, the post butcher at Fort Stanton, as the new sheriff. A huge man of thirty-seven, Copeland was well intended but slow-witted and easily influenced when drinking.[138]

As for Patrón, he was reserving his proverbial powder until the new grand jury was appointed in a few days. As commission chairman, he felt certain he would be named to the jury. It was there he would try to balance the scales in what had become a lopsided fight in favor of the Dolan faction.

After five days of unexplained foot-dragging, Judge Warren Bristol finally impaneled the grand jury on April 13. Fifteen men were selected. As expected, Patrón was appointed to the jury panel. Three of the surplus jurors were designated as alternates, and Dr. Blazer was elected jury foreman.[139]

In his opening charge to the jury, Bristol delivered a stem-winding oration, aimed almost entirely at McSween. Tossing aside all judicial detachment, he brazenly displayed his own partiality in the case against McSween for embezzlement and presented the jury with an accusatory bill of particulars, worthy of a zealous prosecutor, placing at McSween's feet all of the troubles besetting the county.

Only in his closing words did Bristol finally turn to criminal acts by other people that the jury also should consider in its deliberations, devoting a mere sixty words to Tunstall's death. Judge Bristol was hungry for McSween's hide.[140]

However, the grand jurors defiantly repudiated Bristol's charge. With eight other Hispanics on the panel, Patrón undeniably had the most influence over the twelve-man jury. He and most of the other jurors sympathized with McSween's cause and looked upon Judge Bristol as nothing more than a partisan tool of the Dolan faction.

After several days of hearing witnesses from across the county, the jury issued its two reports, noting that "a great portion of testimony taken before us was palpably prejudiced and of a contradictory character." Crisply written and unambiguous, they had all the earmarks of a product by Juan Patrón, a skilled wordsmith.[141] In the case against McSween, the jury reported:

> Your Honor charged us to investigate the case of Alex. A. McSween, Esq., charged with the embezzlement of $10,000 belonging to the estate of Emil Fritz, deceased; this we did but were unable to find any evidence that would justify that accusation. We fully exonerate him of the charge and regret that a spirit of persecution has been shown in the matter.

It was a public rebuke of Judge Bristol for trying to force his prejudiced views upon the jury in the McSween case. The report then continued:

> The murder of John H. Tunstall, for brutality and malice, is without a parallel and without a shadow of justification. By this inhuman act, our county has lost one of our best and most useful men, one who brought intelligence, industry and capital to the development of Lincoln County. We equally condemn the most brutal murder of our late sheriff, William Brady, and George Hindemann.

For the Tunstall killing, Buck Morton and Tom Hill already had been killed by the Regulators, but murder indictments were returned against Jesse Evans, Manuel Segovia (also known as "The Indian") and Frank Rivers, an Evans gang member. James Dolan and Billy Mathews were indicted as accessories.

In the Brady murder, Billy Bonney, Fred Waite, John Middleton and Henry Brown were indicted. Charles Bowdre, alone among the Regulators, was charged with the murder of Buckshot Rogers at Blazer's Mills. Most of the other Regulators, except for the Coe cousins, were named as accessories.

Strangely, the killing of Buck Morton, Frank Baker and William McCloskey by the Regulators escaped any official mention by the grand jury. However, John Riley was indicted for receiving stolen cattle on behalf of the House in what could be seen as veiled payback for shooting Juan Patrón in the back in 1875.

In issuing its April 18 reports, the grand jury also excoriated the governor for fueling violence in the county:

> Had his Excellency, S.B. Axtell, when here, ascertained from the people the cause of our troubles, as he was requested, valuable lives would have been spared our community; especially do we condemn that portion of his proclamation relating to J. B. Wilson as Justice of the Peace. Mr. Wilson acted in good faith as such J. P. over a year. Mr. Brewer, deceased, arrested, as we are informed, some of the alleged murderers of Mr. Tunstall by virtue of warrants issued by Mr. Wilson. The part of the proclamation referred to virtually outlawed Mr. Brewer and posse. In fact, they were hunted in the mountains by our late sheriff with U.S. soldiers. We believe that had the governor done his duty whilst here, these unfortunate occurrences would have been spared us.

McSween emerged as the apparent victor, thanks to Patrón and his fellow jurors. Summing up the proceedings, the *Las Vegas Gazette* declared that the McSween party "had routed the opposition horse, foot and dragoon" even though it "had the moral support of Judge Bristol, District Attorney Rynerson and Governor Axtell's proclamation." The jury's findings left the court in such a chaotic state, no criminal cases came to trial. They were held over to the next term along with the new cases resulting from the grand jury indictments.

CHAPTER 13

The Winds of War

The grand jury indictments of James Dolan and John Riley sent The House into fatal collapse. Dolan announced in the *Mesilla Valley Independent* on April 23 that he and Riley had closed their store because "the condition of affairs now existing in this county is such as to make it unsafe for the undersigned to further continue business...." The closing was temporary, he said, but in reality the House was dead. Within days, Dolan and Riley dissolved their partnership, and Thomas B. Catron, the mighty land baron, took control of all of the House's properties mortgaged to him.[142]

Dolan and Riley were not alone in fearing for their lives. Threatened with death by the Regulators, Lawrence Murphy, their political mentor, had fled to Fort Stanton and was granted safe refuge while preparing to move to Santa Fe.

The grand jury's findings, combined with The House's closing, created a burst of good feelings in Lincoln. On an hour's notice after the court adjourned on April 24, two hundred jubilant citizens from all sections of the county gathered that evening in the same courtroom in a mass meeting called by Patrón. Gavel in hand and facing happy faces, he hammered the meeting to order and nominated five of the town's most respected men as officers of the meeting.[143]

The nominees were unanimously approved as Patrón called off each name: Probate Judge Florencio Gonzales for president, former sheriff Saturnino Baca and County Treasurer Jose Montano for vice presidents and McSween and local merchant Isaac Ellis for secretaries. With officers duly elected, the speeches began.

Judge Gonzales led off with a rousing speech that "was vociferously cheered and interrupted by frequent applause," according to the *Mesilla Valley Independent.* Patrón and Montano followed him with their own remarks, both citing the causes of violence in Lincoln County and suggesting expedient remedies.[144]

A committee consisting of Patrón, cattle baron John Chisum and Avery M. Clenny, who served on the grand jury, was appointed to draft resolutions expressing the general feelings and wishes of the assembled crowd. Patrón, who was as quick with his pen as Billy Bonney was with his pistols, welcomed the task of crafting the resolutions.[145]

With the House gone, Dolan indicted and Lawrence Murphy set to leave Lincoln for good, Patrón viewed it as a harbinger for a new era of peace and prosperity. Here also, he believed, was an opportunity to forge a committed friendship between his people, the Hispanics, and the Anglos.

In his sweeping cursive handwriting, Patrón quickly created a wide-ranging document mixed with praise, condemnation, appreciation, hope and brotherly love. One attending citizen, quoted by the *Mesilla Valley Independent*, summarized it in this way: "I trust that the pledge of friendship and good feeling made this evening in so solemn and appropriate a manner may never be marred or broken."[146] The document read in part:

> *BE IT RESOLVED:*
>
> 1.   That it is the sense of this meeting that our present troubles are only a continuance of old feuds, dating back five or six years, that will now cease as the cause has been removed.
>
> 2.   That the thanks of the people of Lincoln County are hereby due to Lieutenant Colonel Dudley, U.S.A., commanding Fort Stanton, N.M., for his conduct as an officer and a gentleman. That we do consider the day he took command at Fort Stanton important in the history of our county. That we assure him of our appreciation of the intelligent, cautious, and earnest manner in which he has applied himself in ferreting out the cause of our troubles.... His non-partisan conduct and frankness toward the people on one hand and these men on the other is a guarantee that he alone is the commanding officer at Fort Stanton.
>
> 3.   That we condemn without qualification the conduct of our governor, S.B. Axtell, while here in March last. Both his

conduct and proclamation of March 9, 1878, are unworthy of an officer filling his exalted station. His refusal to investigate our troubles stamps him as a little, one-sided partisan. As a result of that proclamation, he is responsible for the loss of life that has occurred in this county since his visit.

4.   That we recognize with expressible pleasure the good and united feeling that binds all our people, Mexicans and Americans, together. We recognize our mutual dependence upon each other, and we pledge our lives and our property to the protection of each other and the maintenance of the laws.

5.   That a vote of thanks be tendered to the United States soldiers, non-commissioned officers and privates, for their commendable conduct while here during the court.

6.   That we thank John H. Copeland for having accepted the office of sheriff and for his important and efficient discharge as such, since he took charge.

7.   That the secretaries of this meeting furnish copies of the proceedings thereof to the President of the United States, to the Honorable Secretary of War, to His Excellency, S. B. Axtell, and that copies thereof be furnished to the "Mesilla Independent" and the "Cimarron News and Press" for publication; and also that they furnish copies for Hon. Florencio Gonzales, Hon. Juan B. Patrón and Isaac Ellis, Esq., who are hereby constituted a committee to wait upon Lieutenant Colonel Dudley, U.S.A., commanding Fort Stanton, N.M., to deliver to him the proceeding in English and Spanish as a token of respect.[147]

The lavish attention given Colonel Nathan A. Dudley was a curious sop. Was it to neutralize the army in the ongoing war or to curry future favor from the new post commander? Dudley had taken command of the post two weeks earlier from Captain George A. Purington, a Dolan partisan openly hostile toward McSween. Whatever the intentions, Patrón and the other leaders knew very little about the officer upon whom they heaped such ingratiating praise.

While considered efficient by army standards, Dudley had his flaws. Stern and arrogant, he commanded mostly through fear and coercion. Worse, he was notorious among his officers as a heavy drinker, causing him to act hastily and beyond bounds when fogged by whiskey. In the coming weeks, McSween would suffer dearly from Dudley's miscalculations.

Despite Patrón's noble efforts to foster harmony in the county, peace was not at hand. Events were colliding that promised renewed fighting. McSween announced that Tunstall's father had posted a five thousand dollar reward for the arrest and conviction of his son's killers, thus reenergizing the restless Regulators to go after the killers. Bitter over the collapse of the House and Dolan's indictment as an accessory to Tunstall's murder, the Dolan gang had fresh cause for revenge. "All agree that a collision is imminent and that it will end in bloodshed," the *Mesilla Valley Independent* correctly prophesized.[148]

For the next sixty days, life for the Regulators was a flurry of shootouts, hard riding and occasional relief at *bailes* wherever their hunt for Tunstall's killers took them. Frank McNab was their new leader. He had obtained a commission as deputy constable from the justice of the peace in nearby San Patricio, thus preserving the group's façade of legality. Warrants in hand, the Regulators were on the hunt again.

Gun battles between the two factions broke out wherever they caught up with each other, from San Patricio in the Ruidoso Valley to the Chisum ranch on the Pecos. Most of the shooting encounters were bloodless stand-offs. However, on April 29, McNab was killed in an ambush nine miles down the Bonito from Lincoln by a self-proclaimed posse of stockmen recruited by Dolan. Two weeks later, the Regulators responded in a raid on a Dolan cow camp, killing Manuel Segovia, who had been in the posse that murdered Tunstall.

At this point, the feud had escalated into open warfare. It consumed everyone in the region, making it almost impossible to remain neutral. Both sides forced settlers to feed and shelter them and on occasion even coerced them at gunpoint to join their gangs.

Throughout it all, Patrón refused to take up arms. He remained dutiful in keeping a steady hand on the levers of county government. Taxes and bills were coming due, and the citizenry deserved to have a functioning government.

On June 1, the Patrón commission learned that the war was slowing the filing of real estate and personal property tax assessments in the county, posing a serious problem if county coffers fell short of money to pay its bills. Confronted with a high number of delinquent filings, the commission levied a punishing twenty-five percent increase on the assessments of delinquent taxpayers.[149]

While the commission punished with one hand, it rewarded with the other. Acting on a petition signed by a majority of county taxpayers, the commissioners obligingly increased the salary of the office of probate judge to two hundred dollars a year. Then, in a twist of irony, Patrón dutifully approved payment to the man who had placed him in the sights of Dolan's gunslingers. District Attorney William Rynerson submitted an affidavit for thirty-five dollars for services in Judge Bristol's courtroom in April. Without dissent, the commission paid him.[150]

The war turned hotter in early June when Dolan returned to Lincoln after a month's stay in Santa Fe where he helped Murphy settle into a new home. In Santa Fe, he leaned on old friends again for help. At his urging and with Rynerson's backing, Governor Axtell on May 28 negated the appointment of John Copeland as sheriff for failing to post a required bond and elevated George W. Peppin, a deputy under Brady, to be the new sheriff. The sheriff's badge belonged to Dolan again.

Peppin quickly assembled a formidable army. It included the usual collection of Dolan henchmen and a gang of eleven ruffians led by John Kinney, a Rio Grande stock thief and thug more notorious than his prodigy Jesse Evans.

Preparing to march on Lincoln, Peppin stationed men everywhere, stalking the roads in and out of Lincoln for the Regulators and making them unsafe for anyone seen as a McSween sympathizer. For Juan Patrón, it created a dangerous situation. He had been summoned to serve as a juror in the Tunstall murder case coming before Judge Bristol in Mesilla on June 17.

In his capacity as commission chairman, Patrón sent an urgent message on June 10 to Colonel Dudley, requesting a military escort to Mesilla for himself and all others subpoenaed to appear in court either as jurors, witnesses or under indictments. "There are armed men waylaying the roads...for the purpose of taking our lives," Patrón said.

Dudley responded the next day by letter, promising Patrón he would furnish a military escort for their protection, provided they produce official affidavits confirming their call to court. Affecting his impartiality in the matter, Dudley said that "parties belonging to either faction now causing the disturbance in Lincoln County will be equally entitled to avail themselves of this guard." In this way, he explained, it denied both sides "an excuse for delaying" the cases coming before the court.[151]

On June 13, Patrón and the others summoned to court assembled at Fort Stanton, where they joined a four-man military escort party that would lead them to Mesilla. Well supplied, each escort had twenty days of rations and one hundred rounds of ammunition to fend off any potential highwaymen intending to murder Patrón or witnesses.

After the court hearing, in which the accused Jesse Evans was freed on bond, Patrón returned home to a town gripped in fear. The peril that open warfare would bring to Lincoln sent residents fleeing. Many abandoned their adobes and farms for safety elsewhere. With Peppin's posse now packed with hired hoodlums like Kinney and his men, Patrón was convinced they were as eager for his death as McSween's.

His fears proved prescient. On the night of June 23, one of Kinney's men, James A. Reese, marched uninvited into Patrón's home, wielding a drawn pistol. "I verily believe I would have been murdered," Patrón wrote Colonel Dudley the next morning, "had Mickey Cronin, not been with me in the room." Colonel Cronin was a close friend and former army man residing in Lincoln.

Shaken by Reese's brazen intrusion, Patrón asked Dudley for temporary protection at Fort Stanton "until I can get through my county business." He explained that "under the present state of affairs in this town, I cannot attend to them." Patrón also suggested he travel to the post with Frank W. Angel, a federal agent who had arrived in Lincoln days earlier to investigate the cause of violence in the county.[152]

Dudley promptly replied the next day, offering a single military escort to the fort, but Patrón was without a horse and had to borrow one from a neighbor to make his way to Fort Stanton the following day. Ever mindful of his duties, he called a hasty meeting of the commissioners to handle one small piece of business before leaving.

The county still owed Sheriff Peppin, a carpenter and brick mason, for constructing a pair of window shutters and a ladder for the public jail he built months before. The commission voted to settle the bill, and Patrón begrudgingly ordered payment to the man whose posse was imperiling his life. Two weeks later, Patrón submitted his own affidavit for supplying the adobe bricks for the jailer's house above the pit jail. It was approved, and he was paid fifty-two dollars.[153]

Such mundane matters may have seemed trivial to some, but to Patrón they held great significance. He saw them as a means of reassuring fellow citizens that their government would not be stilled by the gunfire echoing all around them. The war be damned, he was going to keep the wheels of government turning.

CHAPTER 14

The Big Battle

W hen Patrón decided to take refuge at Fort Stanton, he departed Lincoln in the nick of time. A final showdown between the two warring factions came in mid-July in what would be called "The Five-Day Battle." McSween and his warriors had been dodging the Peppin posse for weeks. Roughing it in the hills, however, was taking its toll on McSween, a real city dweller. Weary from being on the run, he decided to return to the comfort of his home and make a forceful stand against Dolan.

On the night of July 14, McSween and sixty of his warriors galloped into Lincoln and took up strategic positions in Ike Ellis's store and home, the Jose Montano store and McSween's nine-room, U-shaped home facing the Bonito. All three structures had thick adobe walls, providing a sturdy shield against incoming bullets.

McSween's plan was simple. They would lay in wait for Peppin and his posse when they came to serve their arrest warrants. Both ends of town were covered, with McSween and fifteen of his men, including Billy Bonney, barricaded in his home on the west side with the other forty-five men spread inside each of the two stores on the east side.

Dolan and Peppin were encamped in the Wortley Hotel with a few men while another dozen of their men were ensconced in the two-story *torreon,* the town tower. When they learned McSween was back in town in force, Peppin sent a rider into the hills to call back the rest of their men out looking for the Regulators. By dusk, the Dolan forces had reassembled in town, forty strong, including the notorious John Kinney and Jesse Evans.

Gunfire erupted that night and continued sporadically into the next day and night. Hundreds of bullets crisscrossed Lincoln's dusty street, pounding into adobe walls and taking big bites out of the *torreon*. Miraculously, no one was hit. However, the crackling of gunfire echoing around the clock kept citizens cowering inside their homes. Their children, trembling in fear, were hungry and crying, but no one dared to go outside for water, firewood or food.

Heading into the third day, neither side had gained any advantage. But logistics had become a serious problem for McSween and his men. Fresh water was almost gone in McSween's home and the Montano store, and communication between their three scattered fortifications was nearly impossible.

Dolan had his own frustrations too. He was outnumbered in guns, and his attempts to force McSween to surrender had failed miserably. He wanted more firepower to end the standoff. On July 16, Sheriff Peppin obliged him by sending a courier to Fort Stanton with a message requesting Colonel Dudley to lend him a howitzer. Dudley wanted to do so, but declined because the new Posse Comitatus Act that Congress passed a month earlier forbid the U.S. military to interfere in local law enforcement.

Dudley sent his regrets by courier in a message saying that "were I not so circumscribed by laws...I would most gladly give you every man and material at my post to sustain you in your present position." When Private Berry Robinson rode into Lincoln with the entrusted message late that day, the black trooper ran into a hail of rifle fire. As bullets spit up dirt all around him, his horse reared and dumped him. Shaken by the fall, the trooper quickly remounted and raced safely to the Wortley Hotel and delivered the entrusted message to Peppin.[154]

The firing upon a U.S. soldier enraged Dudley. The next day, he sent a board of officers to investigate the matter, and they too were greeted with rifle fire from the flat roof of McSween's home. Decrying the firing upon his soldiers as an "infamous outrage," the colonel rallied his officers and decided that troops were needed in Lincoln to protect its women and children.

On July 19, the fifth day of battle, a military column led by Dudley came into sight to the west of Lincoln as the sun climbed toward its midday zenith. Adorned in full-dress uniforms, the column included four officers, eleven black cavalrymen (Buffalo Soldiers) and twenty-four white infantrymen. Rumbling behind them were an impressive twelve-pounder mountain howitzer and a rapid-fire Gatling gun.

The spiffy appearance of Dudley's entourage looked more like a military unit on parade than one headed into a war zone. But it was in true character for this fifty-two-year-old army commander, known in the ranks as "Gold Lace Dudley," because of his penchant for embellishing his uniform with gold braid and cord.

Lt. Col. Nathan Augustus Monroe Dudley

Before dismounting, Dudley approached both factions and declared he would remain neutral unless his men were fired upon: he was in Lincoln only to protect the women and children. His later deeds, however, would betray that promise.

Dudley immediately shifted the tactical advantage from McSween to Dolan. As his column moved slowly past McSween's home, Peppin's men followed alongside and took up better positions around the besieged lawyer's house. Dudley then encamped in an area across from the Montano store and, aware that McSween's men were barricaded inside, aimed his mighty howitzer at the building's front door.

Not daring to give Dudley any cause to fire the big gun, the defenders inside decided to surrender their position. Concealing their identities as best they could, they bolted from the store, racing east down the street for the Ellis store to rejoin the other McSween fighters.

From his camp, Dudley had a clear line of sight to the Ellis store. He quickly ordered his artillerymen to swing the menacing howitzer at the forty fighters now cramped inside the building. Their weapons silenced by the awesome firepower facing them, the entire force abandoned their bastion and raced across the shallow Bonito for cover in the hills. Peppin and his men gave chase but halted at the river's edge as the escaping McSween men let loose a stream of parting shots.

With the balance of power now in his favor, Peppin made a final attempt to serve warrants on the men inside the McSween home. Deputy Marion Turner, with several other deputies, approached the front of the house and shouted through the windows that he had warrants for McSween's arrest. Refusing to come out, McSween hollered back that he held his own warrants for their arrest. When Turner demanded to see them, Jim French shouted out, with no apologies for his metaphorical French, "Our warrants are in our guns, you cock-sucking sons of bitches." After exchanging a few minutes of vulgar insults, Turner and his men withdrew.[155]

With two-thirds of McSween's men scattered in the hills, Peppin turned his full attention to the Scotsman's house. If four days of shooting couldn't dislodge McSween and his fighters, he would burn them out. That afternoon, one of Peppin's men set fire to the kitchen at the northwest end of the U-shaped house. Being an adobe structure with little wood inside, the flames held but spread slowly from room to room.

By 4 p.m., a column of smoke clouded over the house after flames reached the wooden beams and lattices in the ceiling. The McSween men tucked away in the hills saw it and tried to aid their beleaguered comrades. From the north slopes of the river, they laid down a spray of rifle fire on the possemen, trying to unpin their fighters, choking on smoke inside the burning house. Peppin and his men returned fire from the *torreon,* but it was Dudley who muzzled the Winchesters barking in the hills as he turned the howitzer and Gatling gun in their direction.

By late afternoon, a sense of doom overcame McSween. He was a picture of a defeated man, slouched in a corner, head down and in a stupor as his house burned down around him. Billy Bonney, on the other hand, was as restless as a caged cat. While others tried to slow the fire by ripping up the wooden floor, Bonney scampered about planning an escape. Shaking McSween to his senses, Billy jerked him to his feet and told him they *had* to make a break for it at first darkness if they were to save their lives.

Next, they sent Sue to join her sister and children and the Ealys in the Tunstall store, next door. When Sue reached the store, possemen were inside about to torch it, too. Sue helped the Ealys grab their possessions and carry them outside. At their request, Dudley provided a wagon and soldiers to move their belongings about two hundred yards east to Patrón's vacant house, which sat next to the Montano store. The final wagonload included Sue's precious organ, Ealy's medical books and a sack of flour.[156]

In the meantime, Bonney laid out his plan to McSween. At first darkness, he and four other men would slip out of the last room still free of fire and make a run for the Bonito. This would draw gunfire from Peppin's men, allowing McSween and the others to follow and bolt for the river and its shielding tree line.

At about 9 p.m., Bonney and his group safely crept out of the house into the shadows of the night. In single file, they started into the open, now illuminated by the flames. Peppin's posse spotted them and delivered heavy fire. Each runner broke into a zigzag trying to dodge the spray of bullets. Morris fell dead in front of Bonney just moments before the rest reached the river. Starved for breath, Jim French, Tom Folliard, Jose Chavez y Chavez and Bonney rested amid the trees across the river.[157]

When McSween and the rest of his fighters left the house, they were greeted by a deadly spray of bullets, pinning them down in the backyard. Some dove into the chicken coop for cover. Others crouched tightly against the walls of the house. As for McSween, his courage had hit empty. He hollered out that he wanted to surrender.

Deputy Robert Beckwith and three other men emerged into the open and approached the beleaguered Scotsman. When Beckwith faced McSween at the kitchen doorway to serve the arrest warrant, a defiant McSween suddenly bellowed, "I will never surrender," surprising everyone.[158]

Gunfire erupted on both sides, and the exchange quickly turned into a shooting frenzy. Men shot blindly and at close range, with lead whistling in every direction across the darkened yard. Beckwith was the first to fall, catching a ball in the corner of his left eye and another in the wrist. He died instantly.

Within seconds, five bullets hammered into McSween, and his riddled body fell on top of Beckwith. As he toppled, two of his defenders, Vincente Romero and Francisco Zamora, absorbed fatal shots and collapsed next to their fallen leader. Two other defenders were severely wounded. Yginio Salazar, a teenager, took a bullet in the back and one in the shoulder but remained conscious. Feigning death while absorbing a nasty kick by John Kinney to verify he was dead, young Salazar later dragged himself to a friend's home and survived. The other wounded defender, Ignacio Gonzales, caught a slug in the arm, leaving him bleeding badly. But he managed to escape the yard in all the confusion, scampering across the Bonito with the rest of the McSween defenders.

When daylight broke on July 20, the previous night's carnage produced a grim scene in the yard outside the smoking ruins of the McSween house. Five bloodied bodies lay strewn like scattered cordwood. Chickens pecked at the corpses until they were booted away. Then, the bodies were covered and carried inside the Tunstall store for a coroner's jury to examine.

After the jury's verdict, Sheriff Peppin released the bodies. Beckwith was carried away by friends, and arrangements were made for him to be buried in the Fort Stanton cemetery. Friends also recovered the bodies of Zamora and Romero, as did the friends of Morris.

That afternoon, McSween was buried without ceremony in a grave dug by his loyal black servant, Sebrian Bates. The Scotsman was laid to rest next to John Tunstall, his Englishman friend and partner. Now together in the everlasting, their remaining bones lay silently in a field east of the store that brought them not great wealth, but tragic death. Sue McSween never went to see her husband after he was killed. Nor did she attend his burial, according to the *Mesilla News*.[159]

CHAPTER 15

Violence Continues

Alexander McSween's death should have put an end to the Lincoln County War. Dolan was bankrupt. His competition was dead and buried. With both of their enterprises in ruins, there was nothing more to fight over. But old hostilities died slowly.

Although the Regulators and the Peppin posse formally dissolved after the Five-Day Battle, men from both sides decided to stay in the county. Billy Bonney and his pals remained to avenge the killing of Tunstall and McSween and to watch over Sue McSween, fraught with worry that Dolan or Dudley wanted her killed.

The nastiest of Peppin's posse stayed behind for a different reason. Among the possemen were John Kinney, Jesse Evans and their rapacious gangs who saw a country ripe for taking what they wanted and for shooting anyone who tried to stop them. With Colonel Dudley's troops penned in at their post by congressional dictum and Sheriff Peppin afraid to venture beyond sight of Fort Stanton, there was no visible law enforcement in Lincoln County.

Busy settling her husband's estate, Sue McSween remained in Patrón's house through August under the protection of Bonney's men. Charlie Bowdre, Doc Scurlock and Jim French took turns sleeping in front of the Patrón house every night to calm the overwrought widow. "I guess we owed it to the widow of old penny pincher Mac," recalled French, "but she never even thanked us, never even offered us breakfast."[160]

While Sue sat safely ensconced in his home, Patrón remained at Fort Stanton to preserve his own life. However, troubling news reached him about a random savagery that had descended upon his county. A new gang of thugs from Texas had blown into the area, creating appalling havoc in the small settlements along the Hondo, Bonito and Ruidoso. The gang was led by John Selman, an escaped criminal with a record of brutal violence that made Kinney and Evans look like Boy Scouts.

Throughout August and September, the Selman Scouts, as they liked to call themselves, plundered at will with a cruel barbarity never seen before in Lincoln County. With the Evans and Kinney gangs riding with them as the Wrestlers, Selman and his brutes raped, killed, maimed and drove off stock with impunity. On a single September day, they left a horrifying trail of unbelievable destruction along the Hondo and Bonito. A family was brutalized, two women dragged away from husbands and raped, three men riddled with bullets while cutting hay and a retarded teenage boy offering them watermelons shot in the head, chest and belly. The populace cried out for help.[161]

Stuck at Fort Stanton, Patrón felt politically impotent to deal with the horrors engulfing his county. Something had to be done, and he turned to an old friend and mentor for help. Saturnino Baca had brought his family to the army post at the height of the Five-Day Battle to ensure the safety of his wife and their newborn child. Because the Baca home was next to the *torreon,* it sat dangerously in the line of fire between the two warring factions.

Huddled with his old friend in cramped quarters, Patrón proposed that county officials formally petition Governor Axtell for help in getting the army involved. With Baca's concurrence, Patrón wrote the strongest possible appeal to the governor and sent Baca to round up officials to sign the petition and go to Santa Fe to lay it before Axtell.

Certain that his signing the petition would only torpedo the mission since he previously had criticized Axtell's mishandling of the war, Patrón wisely kept his name off the document. While Baca rode about gathering signatures across the county, Dolan had convinced Colonel Dudley that Patrón had been a McSween spy at the outset of the big battle.

Dudley bluntly confronted Patrón and accused him of spying on his movements and actions. Patrón protested he was not a spy, but Dudley rudely ordered him off the post. Returning to Lincoln was not an option for Patrón. It was unsafe there, and Sue McSween still occupied his house. Choosing to get far away from Lincoln, Patrón began a four-day ride north to Las Vegas.[162]

By then, Baca, a former legislator and currently county school commissioner, had assembled a prominent delegation of county officials. With the Patrón petition in hand, Baca, Probate Judge Florencio Gonzales, County Treasurer Jose Montano and Precinct Four Justice of the Peace George Kimbrell reached Santa Fe on August 20. Axtell received the Lincoln delegation and promptly forwarded the petition to President Hayes with his endorsement. Pointing out that New Mexico had no militia and lacked the dollars to organize one, the governor declared that only federal troops could "end this horrible state of affairs."[163]

The governor's endorsement was seen as lacking and not forceful enough for President Hayes to risk congressional anger by ordering military intervention in Lincoln County. His administration by then had lost all confidence in Axtell because of the governor's flawed handling of the county's troubles. Within two weeks, Axtell was replaced by General Lew Wallace as the new governor.

While Patrón's petition missed its mark in bringing the military to the rescue of his people, it hastened Axtell's departure and left Dolan and his frontier ruffians without a loyal partisan in the governor's office. To Patrón's delight, the new governor was no party hack like Axtell and others who had been sent by presidents to run the remote territory.

At fifty-one, Wallace had garnered a record of genuine distinction. He was a respected soldier, lawyer, politician, author and scholar. During the Civil War, he quickly climbed to the rank of major general by the age of thirty-four, becoming one of the youngest in the Union Army. After the war, he served on the court-martial that tried the Lincoln conspirators and presided over the court that convicted the commander of the notorious confederate prison at Andersonville. By any measure, Wallace brought to the office an intellect and range of abilities unrivaled by any of his predecessors. With piercing dark eyes set deep in a weathered face, festooned with a thick hanging mustache and beard, Wallace stood tall, slender and clutched in military bearing. He looked and acted like a governor.

Without ceremony, he was sworn in on Monday morning, September 30. He delved into his new duties with a fervor unseen before in the governor's office. Within five days he had gathered evidence to call for a daring step. With the army, the courts, the sheriff and U.S. marshal declared impotent by their own admission and the territory without a militia, Wallace urged President Hayes to declare Lincoln County to be in a state of insurrection and impose martial law.

Former Governor Lew Wallace in 1886

President Hayes reacted quickly to Wallace's appeal but judged that martial law was politically unacceptable in view of the new Posse Comitatus Act. To use troops to catch outlaws was one thing, but to have them try, convict and sentence them by a military commission under martial law was too politically distasteful for Hayes.

On October 7, he issued a proclamation that went halfway. He commanded all citizens in Lincoln County to cease all lawless acts and "to disperse and return peacefully to their respective abodes by noon on the thirteenth day of October." After that date, he decreed, the army could again legally furnish troops to support civil authorities in the search for resistant lawbreakers. Wallace was disappointed by Hayes's fence straddling but would make do with what was given him.[164]

Two weeks before Wallace took over the Palace of the Governors, Sue McSween had gathered her few belongings and fled to Las Vegas, where her sister Elizabeth's husband and former McSween law partner, David Shield, had set up a new law practice. With Sue gone from his house and a new governor in Santa Fe, Juan Patrón returned to Lincoln in early October and resumed his county duties.

The county commission had been idle since Patrón's departure in mid-July, and time was running short in preparing for the important November 5 elections. Patrón hastily gathered the commission on October 13. It promptly appointed the boards of registration for each of the county's six precincts and named the necessary election judges.[165]

Patrón wanted the elections to run smoothly because voters, for the first time in years, had an opportunity to elect a decent, competent sheriff. The favored candidate was thirty-seven-year-old George Kimbrell, the justice of the peace in Precinct Four. Known as a sensible, honest and fearless man who would show no favor, Kimbrell represented a great improvement over both Copeland and Peppin.

Patrón decided not to stand for reelection that November. Pensive hours at Fort Stanton and Las Vegas had provided him time to ponder his future. Life for him had become too precarious in Lincoln. At age twenty-five, Patrón decided it was time to consider marriage and starting a family somewhere other than in Lincoln. Whatever ensued in Lincoln County in the coming year, Patrón decided, he would formally court Beatriz Labadie in Santa Rosa, far from Lincoln.

But horrors continued across the land. Within days of Patrón's return to Lincoln, word reached town of the brutal slaughter of a Hispanic family of nine by the Selman Scouts at a settlement north of Roswell. The news ignited such deep indignation in Patrón that he took up arms and formed a citizens' posse to hunt down the murderers.

Accounts of the posse's activities are vague. One account by Maurice Fulton in his history of the Lincoln County War states that the Patrón posse killed two men, reportedly members of the Selman gang, somewhere between Fort Sumner and Lloyd's Crossing, a few miles north of Roswell. A report from Colonel Dudley to Wallace told of ten murders in the same period, including two men killed by the Patrón posse, one of whom was hung near Puerto de Luna.[166]

Captain Henry H. Carroll, a cavalry company commander at Fort Stanton, also had been alerted to the appearance of Patrón and his posse near Roswell in a letter dated October 11, 1878, from army sergeant George Davis. "There are a great many armed men here every day," Davis wrote. "They claim to belong to the Lincoln outfit. Juan Patrón will be down from [Lincoln] this evening with twenty-six men. They say that they will then have about sixty men and intend to start for Seven Rivers tonight or in the morning. The people are very uneasy for fear that they will be murdered."[167]

The Selman and Kinney gangs had been rustling cattle in the Seven Rivers area for weeks. Whether the Patrón posse ever caught up with the gangs in the Pecos Valley south of Roswell is lost in history. However, President Hayes's proclamation finally unleashed the troops at Fort Stanton to chase after outlaws and confine them. In late October, a cavalry company led by Captain Carroll was dispatched to Roswell to hunt down the busy cattle thieves known as the Wrestlers.

Conscientious and a seasoned soldier, Carroll had climbed up from the ranks and had proved himself a good officer. While combing the frozen valleys of the Pecos for cattle thieves that winter, Carroll and his men found the bones of the nine Hispanics whose deaths Patrón had tried to avenge. The killers were John, Jim, Tom and Bill Jones and John Collins, all former riders in the Peppin posse paid for by James Dolan. They avoided prosecution by claiming they killed the Hispanics for supposedly slaying a friend of the Jones family. The scene Carroll's troopers came upon that day was masked in macabre humor. They found the skeleton of one, a teenage boy, propped against a tree. The skull had fallen off and lay nearby with a cigar stuffed in its mouth.[168]

The Wrestlers were not the only ones stripping cattle from the herds of innocent ranchers. Billy Bonney and his pals had resumed old habits after Sue McSween left Lincoln. No longer tied down as her protectors, they left Lincoln and began stealing horses and cattle again. Before leaving, cousins Frank and George Coe invited Billy to join them in forsaking the outlaw life, but the Kid replied, "Well boys, you may do exactly as you please. I am off now, with any of my *compadres* who will follow me. I need *dinero*. I am broke, fellows, and I need to make a killing."[169]

Charles Fritz's ranch east of Lincoln was the first hit by Billy and his boys. They ran off with fifteen horses and one hundred and fifty cattle to begin a herd they expanded near Fort Sumner and eventually sold in the Texas Panhandle. For the next few months, Billy, Charlie Bowdre and Doc Scurlock spent most of their time around Fort Sumner, separating horses from the Indians by day and dealing three-card monte in saloons by night.

By now, Billy was looked upon as the recognized leader of the former Regulators who had turned to open outlawry for their living. Unlike the savagery practiced by John Selman and his henchmen, Bonney and his gang limited their illegal pursuits to stealing horses and cattle, without regard to ownership. But wherever they rode, Billy and his men remained on constant lookout for Peppin's former possemen. The Wrestlers were just as anxious to run up on the former Regulators. Fortunately for both sides, they seemed unable to find each other.

While general lawlessness remained rampant throughout the county, the old Dolan-McSween feud heated up again after Sue McSween returned to Lincoln in December. She brought with her a brash young lawyer named Huston Chapman, whom she hired in Las Vegas to help settle her husband's estate. They took up residence in Santurnino Baca's former home, which was owned by the McSweens.

Sickly and with an arm missing, Chapman was an excitable, pushy young man with a flair for penning verbose letters sprinkled with hyperbole. His fiery missives were aimed primarily at Governor Wallace, accusing Colonel Dudley and Sheriff Peppin of murder and arson in the death of Alexander McSween. Taking up Sue's cause, Chapman demanded that Dudley be removed from command and that he and Peppin face criminal charges. By December 7, Wallace also concluded that Dudley should go and recommended that the army relieve Dudley of his command but was promptly rebuffed by the Hayes Administration.

While Chapman continued to agitate for Dudley's head to anyone who would listen, his "hysterical" persistence had stirred old rivalries. In mid-February, combustible elements had gathered in Lincoln. Prominent Regulators like Billy Bonney, Doc Scurlock, Charley Bowdre and a new acolyte, Tom Folliard, were back in town. And their old foe James Dolan had returned, too, up from the Pecos with Jesse Evans and a dangerous cattle driver named William A. "Billy" Campbell.

Dolan had hired Campbell as chief herder to drive the cattle he had turned over to Thomas Catron to Fort Stanton. Hosting a fierce face with a huge brown mustache, Campbell looked mean. Easily offended, he had a vile temper and was quick to use his fire iron in reply to the slightest umbrage. Even his cowboys were afraid to cross him.

While bounding from one old haunt to another, Bonney let the word out he was tired of ducking arrest warrants and tired of fighting and running from the Dolan gang. Taking up the role of peacemaker, he sent a message to Jesse Evans, who was with Dolan at Fort Stanton, asking if the Dolan people wanted war or peace. The reply came back that Dolan, Evans and their boys would come to Lincoln that night and talk over the question.

Though the number of men is uncertain, the antagonists gathered in town the night of February 18, exactly one year after John Tunstall's murder. From behind opposing walls, they hesitantly advanced into the main street and began their parlay. The opening mood was hostile. Evans claimed the Kid was impossible to deal with and should be killed on the spot, according to the *Mesilla Valley Independent*. "I don't care to open negotiations with a fight," the Kid shouted back, "but if you'll come at me three at a time, I'll whip the whole bunch of you."[170]

Calmer minds eventually prevailed. Edgar Walz, one of Dolan's men, cooled down the talk, and the boys holstered their testosterone. The opposing leaders shook hands and walked together to a saloon to forge a peace treaty. Sitting with Bonney were Doc Scurlock, Tom Folliard, George Bowers and Jose Salazar. Facing them across the table were Dolan, Evans, Walz, Billy Mathews and the trigger-happy Billy Campbell.

After some discussion, the pact was put into writing. It stipulated five points: that no one of either party would kill anyone from the other without first serving notice of withdrawing from the treaty; that persons who had acted as "friends" of both parties were included in the treaty and were not to be molested; that no army officer or soldier would be killed for any past offense; that neither party would testify against the other in any civil prosecution; that each party would give aid to individual members of the other in resisting arrest and, if arrested, secure their release; that anyone who failed to live up to the compact would be killed on sight.[171]

Their scribbled treaty reflected the coda of all frontier gunslingers: *Cross Me and You Die.* It could well have served as an apt title for their compact.

Pleased with their peace accord, the boys toasted their newfound friendship with a round a drinks, followed by many more rounds as they staggered from one drinking hall to another. By 10 p.m., they were roaring drunk, and their next stop was at the home and store of Juan Patrón, who also operated a small bar. Patrón had arrived in town earlier from Las Vegas with Huston Chapman.

No sooner had the noisy celebrants entered the house a boozed-up Billy Campbell yanked out his Colt pistol and aimed it at Patrón. Startled and dragging his lame left leg, Patrón scuttled behind some others in the party and avoided being killed. Sensing that blood was about to be spilled, Bonney convinced the gang to move on.

Ashen-faced and trembling, Patrón watched the drunken group spill out onto the frozen street and stumble toward Frank McCullum's new saloon and eating house, built recently next to the ruins of the McSween house. Patrón had to wonder: was Campbell's threat on his life just a drunken impulse or was he on an assassin's mission?

Lurching toward their next watering hole, the Dolan-Bonney bunch encountered Huston Chapman in front of the courthouse. Bone tired from a long ride, the unarmed lawyer's face was bandaged with a poultice to ease a severe toothache. Campbell was the first to reach Chapman and demanded his name.

"My name is Chapman," he said crisply, "and I am attending to my business."

Campbell angrily commanded, "Then you dance," drawing his pistol and punching it into Chapman's breast.

"I don't propose to dance for a drunken mob," Chapman snapped, asking, "Am I talking to Mr. Dolan?"

"No," replied Jesse Evans, "but you're talking to damn good friends of his."[172]

Dolan, standing ten feet behind Campbell, fired a shot into the street, causing Campbell's trigger finger to tighten instinctively.

"My God, I am killed." Chapman gasped as Campbell's bullet plunged through his heart. As he fell dead, his coat caught fire from the powder flash of Campbell's pistol. Turning away from the inflamed corpse, Campbell led the carousing gang to McCullum's eatery, loudly proclaiming he had "promised my God and Colonel Dudley that he would kill Chapman, and now he had done it."[173]

Over an oyster supper at McCullums, Dolan and Campbell conspired to make the Chapman killing look like self-defense. They handed a pistol to Edgar Walz and told him to put it into the dead lawyer's hand. When Walz declined, Bonney grabbed the gun and went outside. Tucking the gun under his waistband, he darted past Chapman's scorched body to the Ellis store where Folliard held their horses, and the two galloped off to San Patricio.

The volatile mood of Dolan and his boys had troubled Billy since Campbell's attempt on Patrón's life. When the group encountered Chapman, he sensed a killing was coming and tried to break away, but Jesse Evans held him and forced him to watch. With Chapman's death, Bonney had good reason to hustle out of town. Sheriff Kimbrell carried arrest warrants for him and had spotted him in town earlier in the day. Bonney didn't want to be around when Kimbrell returned later that night with a military posse to help arrest him.

Shortly after Bonney's departure, Kimbrell and twenty cavalrymen headed by Lieutenant Byron Dawson arrived in town. After a futile search for Bonney, the troopers lifted Chapman's charred body from the street at about midnight and took it into the courthouse. Then the soldiers departed for their post.

The next day, Patrón drafted a petition, signed by every citizen in

Lincoln at the time, urging Dudley to station troops in town immediately. Kimbrell attached the petition to his own formal request and rushed the papers to Fort Stanton. Within hours, Lieutenant Goodwin and a detachment of soldiers, towing a Gatling gun, rode into Lincoln and encamped in the old Tunstall store.[174]

Earlier in the day, Huston Chapman's body was laid to rest in the McSween cemetery east of the Tunstall store.

Colonel Dudley and Billy Campbell had a known but unexplained relationship. In November, Dudley had summoned Campbell to Fort Stanton for a conversation after Campbell had delivered the Catron herd to the nearby Mescalero reservation. The purpose of their talk was never revealed. In his investigation of Chapman's death, Governor Wallace collected evidence that was damning to Dudley. He found that on the night of the killing, Dolan returned to Fort Stanton, obtained a "loan" of fifty dollars from Dudley and then passed it on to Campbell. The reason for this money exchange has been a tantalizing mystery to historians ever since.[175]

Whether Patrón was on a possible Campbell "hit" list is pure conjecture also. In the months preceding the outlaws' pact, Patrón had established a close association with Chapman as Sue McSween's new lawyer. Both men had become involved in the administering of John Tunstall's estate. As a result, Patrón often was seen with Chapman in town, and they traveled together between Las Vegas and Lincoln. It's possible that Dudley, outraged at Chapman's relentless attacks on him, held that any friend of Chapman's stood as an enemy of his, making Patrón a possible target, *if* Campbell were a hired killer.

Patrón's connection to Chapman began the previous December. After Tunstall's death, his ranch foreman, Robert Widenmann, mortgaged the Englishman's estate to secure bondsmen as the appointed administrator of the estate. The bondsmen were Patrón, Jose Montano, John Copeland and Francisco Romero y Valencia. Probating the estate, however, had been in limbo since mid-June, when Widenmann went to Mesilla to testify in the Tunstall murder case and decided not to return to Lincoln. Frustrated by the delay, the bondsmen served notice that they planned to remove Widenmann as administrator. Chapman learned about their plan, stepped in and proposed that Mrs. McSween be appointed administratrix, replacing Widenmann.

Susan McSween took her oath as administratrix soon after her return to Lincoln in December. Serving as her bondsmen were Patrón, Montano, Copeland and A. J. Ballard. Isaac Ellis and Montano were appointed as appraisers, as they were for McSween's estate. In their January 16 report, Tunstall's personal property was valued at five hundred and thirty-five dollars. Collectible notes amounted to thirty-nine hundred dollars while uncollectible notes totaled fourteen hundred and forty-two dollars. His real estate, including a half-interest in the store, the Feliz ranch land and the George van Sickle ranch, totaled thirteen hundred dollars.

Before his death, Chapman had lectured Wallace, often in harsh tones, to come to Lincoln and sort out the county's troubles, but the governor had continued to procrastinate. What the young lawyer failed to achieve in life, he accomplished in death. When word reached Wallace of Chapman's death, he was told the county was in a near panic because the old warring factions had gathered again. Wallace finally decided, after four and a half months in office, he would go to Lincoln immediately. Although uncertain of the remedy, he would endeavor to restore order as President Hayes expected him to do.

CHAPTER 16

Lincoln County Rifles

⟡⟡⟡⟡⟡

Governor Wallace arrived in Lincoln on March 6, 1879. He had traveled from Santa Fe with Colonel Edward Hatch, the military commander of New Mexico. Both were veterans of the Civil War and enjoyed an amiable relationship. They also shared a mutual disdain for Colonel Dudley and agreed during their travel that he should be relieved of command.

On his arrival, Wallace settled into quarters at Jose Montano's home, while Hatch proceeded to Fort Stanton to inspect the post. The next morning, Wallace called on Juan Patrón, whom he knew as a former speaker of the house and respected leader of the local populace. As the two walked about town, Wallace queried citizens about Dudley's role in the Five-Day Battle. Most held him responsible for McSween's death and believed he also was complicit in Chapman's death. Wallace concluded that Dudley was so entangled in local animosities he would be a detriment to any effort to restore order. Dudley had to go.

With documentation in hand, Wallace rode the following day to Fort Stanton and presented his case to Colonel Hatch, who reacted quickly. Hatch immediately issued orders relieving Dudley of command. Then the governor and the colonel passed the afternoon over a celebration dinner given at the post. Afterward, Wallace returned to Lincoln where Patrón assembled a public meeting in which the governor boasted he had accomplished "the best day's work ever done for the citizens of Lincoln County."[176]

As expected, Dudley reacted with explosive rage. He demanded to be heard, but neither Wallace nor Hatch would take time to talk to him. Dudley had been summarily discharged of his post without a chance to defend himself. Rightly or wrongly, Dudley was out, and Wallace had taken over the campaign to restore peace in the county.

For his campaign to succeed, Wallace needed a post commander with whom he could work in harmony. Captain George Purington was second in command but was on leave in Ohio. Fortunately for Wallace, the command devolved on to the next senior officer, Captain Henry Carroll, the dogged troop commander who had recaptured the Tunstall cattle from the Wrestlers. An able officer and well liked by the citizens, Carroll proved to be a worthy ally to Wallace.

With an energy heretofore reserved for writing the final chapters of his biblical epic *Ben Hur,* the governor devised a quick, simple plan: root out the cattle rustlers along the Pecos and round up all of the outlaws who had terrorized the county in the past year. In executing the plan, Captain Carroll was asked to arrest everyone herding cattle that could not prove ownership by registered brand or bill of sale. The captured cattle were to be entrusted to John Newcomb, whom Wallace titled "Cattle Keeper of the County."

As for the outlaws, Justice John Wilson provided Wallace with a list of thirty-five names that the governor turned over to Carroll on March 11 and asked that they be found and arrested. The list was a bona fide "who's who" of the Lincoln County War, including Regulators Bonney, Waite, Bowdre, Scurlock and French plus their wartime enemies Dolan, Evans and Mathews. John Selman and the Wrestlers also were listed, as were notorious cowmen such as the Jones brothers, Buck Powell, Marion Turner and Roscoe "Rustling Bob" Bryant.[177]

Wallace also wanted the men involved in the Chapman murder, namely Billy Campbell, Dolan, Bonney and Folliard. At Wallace's request, Carroll sent out two detachments. One rode north twenty miles to Las Tablas to hunt for Bonney and Folliard but returned empty handed. The other detachment found Campbell, Evans and Mathews hiding out at Lawrence Murphy's old ranch, Fairview, and hustled them back to the Fort Stanton guardhouse. Dolan subsequently joined them, not in the stockade but under guard in the comfortable post library, as Wallace instructed. The governor hoped to sway Dolan to testify against his friends in April when Judge Bristol held district court in Lincoln.

Captain Carroll persisted in the search for others on Wallace's list. His patrols diligently combed the high hills and river valleys, rounding up a mix of desperados, rustlers and old fighters from the McSween and Dolan factions. Wallace was pleased. By the close of March, he had a dozen outlaws packed into the post guardhouse, which a *Mesilla Valley Independent* reporter later described as "a Bastille crowded with civil prisoners."[178]

While Carroll's roundup of outlaws remained ongoing, Captain George Purington returned from leave and, being senior to Captain Carroll, assumed command of the post. Mulish and an unabashed supporter of the Dolan faction, Purington would prove to be Wallace's worst nightmare.

At every turn, Purington delighted in thwarting Wallace's requests. Ever unyielding, he pointed to army regulations to deny or postpone the governor's appeals, be they for ammunition, supplies or troops to hunt down outlaws. Purington became so uncooperative that Wallace complained to Secretary of Interior Schurz that the "military do not enter heartily into the work requested of them."[179]

Meanwhile, rumors swirled within Lincoln that Evans and Campbell were almost certain to make a break from the post guardhouse. They had busted out of jails many times before. Troubled by the talk, Wallace appealed to Colonel Hatch to ensure "that these prisoners be held securely," declaring he could not rely on Purington to do so.

Purington wasn't Wallace's only worry. Dolan showed no willingness to testify against his friends, and most people still feared retributions if they signed affidavits against the outlaws. "The truth is," Wallace wrote Hatch, "the people here are so intimidated that some days will have to pass before they can be screwed up to the point of making the necessary affidavits."[180]

As Wallace's hopes faded, a turn of good luck came his way. A messenger brought him a letter, dated March 13, from Billy Bonney, who wrote, "I was present when Mr. Chapman was murdered and know who did it." However, he continued, "I have indictments against me for things that happened in the last Lincoln County War and am afraid to give up because my enemies would kill me." If Wallace annulled the indictments, Bonney would testify.[181]

Wallace scribbled a hasty reply and handed it to the waiting messenger. He directed Bonney, "Come to the house of old Squire Wilson at nine (9) o'clock next Monday night alone. Follow along foot of the mountain south of town, come in on that side and knock at the east door. I have authority to exempt you from prosecution, if you will testify to what you say you know."

On that Monday night of March 17, the governor and the young outlaw met in Squire Wilson's crude jacal. No two more dissimilar men could have faced each other: the distinguished soldier-statesman and scholar ready to make a deal with a rumpled young outlaw destined to become a lasting legend in the folklore of the West.

Wallace described the drama of the meeting in an Indianapolis *World* interview on June 8, 1902. As he and Wilson sat in a room dimly lit by a coal oil lamp, they tensely waited for the soft knock on the door. Billy entered hesitantly with a rifle in one hand and six-shooter in the other. When he saw no one else was present, he relaxed and lowered his weapons.

Their talk produced an agreement: Billy would submit to a staged arrest by Sheriff George Kimbrell, remain in jail until the grand jury met, and identify Chapman's murderers. In return, Wallace said, "I will let you go scot free, with a pardon in your pocket for all your misdeeds." Billy left as noiselessly as he had arrived.[182]

Doubting that Purington would ensure Evans's and Campbell's capture and frustrated by his foot-dragging, Wallace took military matters into his own hands. He turned to the one man in Lincoln whom he had come to trust most. On March 15, he directed Juan Patrón to organize and lead a militia company called The Lincoln County Rifles. Its sole mission was to assist civil authorities in repressing violence and restoring order. Wallace hoped its presence also would restore the people's confidence in feeling protected at home and in the fields.[183]

Wallace believed fully in local militias, having enlisted at age nineteen in the Marion Rifles of Indianapolis in 1846. From that group, he organized a militia troop to fight in the Mexican War and eventually reached the rank of Major General in the 11th Indiana Volunteer Infantry.

With military precision, Wallace instructed Patrón on the size, composition and mission of the militia company he desired. It was to have at least thirty-two men but no more than sixty.

To abate any appearance of a militia loaded with local partisans, the governor directed Patrón to select men as far from the Lincoln precinct as possible. He expected them to be law-abiding, able-bodied volunteers of good character and to have their own weapons and horses.

As for its preparedness, Wallace wanted the company ready to ride on a moment's notice. Whenever called out, the riflemen's daily subsistence, including cartridges, was to be at public expense, and an exact accounting required of Patrón. "Extravagant purchases," Wallace warned, "will not be allowed or recommended for payment."

Obedient to Wallace's instructions, the new captain took to the task immediately. Within three days, Patrón assembled a fifty-four-man militia of volunteers ready for duty. He signed on Ben Ellis as his first lieutenant and Martin Sanchez as second lieutenant. For his sergeants, Patrón chose Camillo Nunez, Elias Gray, Ramon Montoya and Estelano Sanchez. He selected for his corporals Trinidad Vigil, Fernando Herrera, Jesus Rodriquez and Juan Pedro Torres. Patrón prepared a roll bearing the name and address of each volunteer and forwarded a copy to Wallace.[184]

Since Patrón and his two lieutenants resided in Lincoln and were known to be McSween supporters, some citizens questioned whether the militia could carry out its mission with impartiality. Wallace had tried to allay such doubts by insisting that as many of the militiamen as possible reside outside the Lincoln precinct. To that extent, Patrón followed Wallace's orders as best he could. Of the fifty-one non-officer militiamen enrolled, only ten lived in Lincoln.

To its detractors like Jimmy Dolan, his hired outlaws and pouting Fort Stanton officers, Wallace's nascent militia quickly earned the contemptuous sobriquet of "The Governor's Heel-flies," the same derisive dubbing given to Texas's inglorious Home Guards during the Civil War.[185]

However, Patrón had his militia ready none too soon. In the pre-dawn hours of March 19, Wallace was awakened at his encampment in Lincoln and told that Jesse Evans and Billy Campbell had escaped from the Fort Stanton guardhouse. Evans had persuaded the duo's posted guard, a young recruit called "Texas Jack," to desert and ride off with them into the mountains.

Wallace was furious. He knew it would be wasted time to ask Purrington for help in recapturing the escaped outlaws. Immediately, the governor dispatched the following note to Patrón:

> Be good enough to send word to all your men to turn out as soon as possible to join in the hunt for Jesse Evans and William Campbell, who escaped from Fort Stanton last night. Say to your men that, as Governor of New Mexico, I offer a reward of $1,000 for Evans and Campbell.[186]

The escape could not have come at a more critical time. With Evans and Campbell on the loose, Wallace feared Bonney would bolt from their deal. But, loyal to his word, Billy surrendered to Sheriff George Kimbrell and his posse on the next day. Billy brought with him his inseparable friend, Tom Folliard, a husky lad who stood over six feet tall and weighed two hundred pounds.

Billy and Folliard had met while working as ranch hands at Frank Coe's place on the Ruidoso. Billy looked after Folliard like an older brother and taught him how to handle a six-shooter. After some practice, his acolyte could shoot as well as Billy. Both were good natured and fun loving. At the sound of Mexican music, they often headed for the local *baile*, where Billy delighted in twirling the senoritas while Folliard obediently tended to their horses outside.[187]

Billy anticipated that he and Folliard would be held in the Fort Stanton guardhouse, but Wallace wanted him safe and out of reach of Dolan's murderous crew now crowded in the post stockade. Instead, Wallace placed the two young outlaws in the protective custody of Juan Patrón, a man Billy liked and trusted.

Being held at Patrón's was luxurious by comparison. Patrón fed Billy and Folliard well and provided them comfortable bedding. Free to move about in the store, they were guarded by an old friend, Deputy Sheriff Tom Longworth.

"The Kid was in a cheerful mood and appeared contented with his lot," Miguel A. Otero, Jr., wrote later. "They ate heartily and well, smoked the best cigars and played poker with occasional friends who dropped in to see them."

Ever the jokester, Billy honed his tricks while passing time in Patrón's custody. Because he had small hands but big wrists, it was difficult to keep his hands cuffed in irons. "When a friend entered," Otero said, "he would slip his hand from the irons, stretch it out to shake hands, and with a bright smile remark, 'You don't get a chance to steal my jewelry, old man.'"[188]

Wallace also made a visit—not to socialize but to collect information. On the Sunday night of March 23, the patrician governor and the scruffy outlaw met face-to-face for the second time. As Wallace took copious notes, Bonney poured out a long, useful narrative of outlaw activities across the territory that he witnessed or knew about.

Admiringly curious about Billy's good marksmanship with a six-shooter, the governor asked if there was "some trick" to his perfect aim. "When I lift my revolver, I tell myself, 'Point with your finger' and unconsciously, it makes the aim certain. I pull the trigger, and the bullet goes true to its mark."[189]

Wallace also was struck by Bonney's popularity in Lincoln. The night before they met, the governor heard singers serenade the prisoner in front of Patrón's home, which sat next door to the Montano home were Wallace was staying. "A precious specimen named 'The Kid,'" he wrote Interior Secretary Schurz, "whom the Sheriff is holding here in the Plaza, as it is called, is an object of tender regard. I heard singing and music the other night; going to the door, I found the minstrels of the village actually serenading the fellow in his prison."[190]

Billy promised Deputy Longworth he would never try to escape as long as he remained at Patrón's house. But a short time later, Longworth brought him bad news. The deputy received orders to place the two prisoners temporarily in Lincoln's dismal dugout jail while they were under summons to appear in district court in April.

"Tom, I've sworn I would never go inside that hole again, alive," Billy told Longworth, who replied, "I don't want to put you...or anyone else there. But those are my orders."

Handcuffed and under guard, Bonney and Folliard walked gloomily across the street to the jailhouse. As Bonney climbed down the ladder into the dirt cellar, he told Longworth, "Tom, I'm going in here because I won't have any trouble with you, but I'd give all I've got if the bastard that gave the order was in your shoes."[191]

While Wallace dealt with Billy, Captain Patrón and his riflemen scoured the countryside in search of Evans and Campbell, going first to locations suggested by Bonney, who knew outlaw practices. "You will never catch those fellows on the roads," Billy warned Wallace in a note before Patrón took to the field. He believed the escapees would try to get provisions first at either Charles Fritz's place or Saturnino Baca's ranch.

"They will stay close until the scouting parties come in." Bonney instructed. "It is not my place to advise you, but I am anxious to have them caught, and perhaps I know how men hide from soldiers better than you. Please excuse me for having so much to say."[192]

For Patrón, riding long hours drove sharp pains into his lame left leg as it slapped hard against the rock-solid saddle. Just hefting himself into the saddle was physically challenging. Pushing the pain aside, he led the riflemen on most patrols, absorbing stabbing jolts as he and his men thundered across rocky terrain looking for the two escaped outlaws. After two days of searching, Patrón and his riflemen returned to Lincoln empty-handed and needing rest.

At Wallace's request, Patrón assembled a fresh squad of nine militiamen to continue the search. Lieutenant Martin Sanchez was sent to Fort Stanton with Wallace's written request for five days of rations and sufficient cartridges. But the governor's old foil, Captain Purington, refused, declaring that he needed written approval from his superiors first, and they were not available.[193]

Captain Patrón refused to be deterred. On his own authority, he requisitioned the needed supplies from local merchant Jose Montano. Led by Lieutenant Sanchez, the squad galloped out of Lincoln the next day, searching the Pecos cow camps stretching from Fort Sumner in the north to south of Roswell. The vigorous search for Evans and Campbell lasted six days. On March 29, Sanchez and his men returned to Lincoln empty handed and tired, their horses reduced to a weak walk. Unless ordered otherwise, Patrón notified Wallace, he was ending the search, now ten days after the two outlaws escaped.

The riflemen fared no worse than the Ninth Cavalry in the search. Both failed to find the two elusive outlaws. However, a cavalry detachment did capture "Texas Jack," the army deserter, obviously lacking the outlaws' skills of eluding a search party. Troopers hustled the recruit back to an already overflowing post stockade.

By April 1, 1879, Wallace conceded that recapturing Evans and Campbell was hopeless. He notified Secretary of Interior Carl Schurz by letter, asking him to read the following personal message to President Hayes: "The desperadoes in this Territory include some of the most noted of their class in the United States. These outlaws cannot be made to quit except by actual war by guns and pistols, not writs and lectures."[194]

Patrón's militia succeeded in one notable capture on April 11. Days before, Wallace had received word that two of Bonney's sidekicks, Charlie Bowdre and J. G. "Doc" Scurlock, were hiding out at a ranch ten miles east of Fort Sumner. They were wanted for the murder of Andrew L. Roberts in April 1878 and had outrun an earlier posse led by Sheriff Kimbrell.

Scurlock's capture resulted from Patrón's stealthy tactics. He and a squad of ten riflemen kept off the trails and rode only at night, approaching the ranch from the west. In pitch darkness, they surprised a sleeping Scurlock, who surrendered without a fight, but Bowdre was long gone. Scurlock was taken back to Patrón's store, joining Bonney and Folliard, already held under guard there. One imagines the lively talks between two well-educated men like Patrón and Scurlock, who came by his nickname "Doc" honestly, having studied medicine in New Orleans. In his lifetime, he also was a farmer, poet, teacher, and later a linguist and reader of the classics—a most unusual gunfighter.

Patrón notified Ben Isaac, his top lieutenant, of Scurlock's capture in a message couriered from Fort Sumner on April 12, providing a picture of life in the field for Patrón and his men while hunting down outlaws.

"I came in here last night from Taiban," Patrón wrote. "

> I got Scurlock but Charlie Bowdre was gone. Day before yesterday, while passing through here, I was informed that a party of nine well-armed and mounted men had passed through Taiban and travelling towards Lincoln along the Pecos River. I immediately notified the troops at Roswell of their approach. I conversed with parties just in from the plains, and they say that those chaps are the same "Rustlers," and before they left Texas, they killed two men and robbed them of everything they had. I will await the buckboard from below to learn what direction they went, and if there is a chance for me, I will go down the river.
>
> Be ready up there [in Lincoln] in case the troops let them pass [Roswell]. Those murderers mean mischief, and if they are not captured or killed, they surely will commit murder and rapine. The troops surely have the best chance to have a *rub* with them since they are notified and posted of their movements. Regards to everybody,"
>
> Signed Juan B. Patrón[195]

After a month in Lincoln, Wallace remained convinced that nothing short of a powerful presence could restrain the cattle rustlers and murderers he had to deal with in New Mexico. With Evans and Campbell still on the loose, he feared that Dolan and the outlaws collected at the fort would try to escape or win release by process of habeas corpus and flee the county.

For the second time, Wallace appealed to President Hayes to declare martial law in Lincoln County but again was refused. He would have to depend on a civil court system in which he had little faith. He doubted that it could muster enough impartial jurors and witnesses to render convictions.

District Court opened on April 14 with Judge Warren Bristol presiding. As Wallace predicted, the appointed grand jury turned in a shameful performance. Nearly all of the jurors were known to be sympathetic to the McSween faction, and it showed in their return of some 200 indictments, most of them against men allied with Dolan's gang.

Only two McSween supporters were indicted. They were Tom Folliard and Sam Smith, who were charged with the theft of Charles Fritz's horses. Folliard, in pleading guilty, was granted immunity under Wallace's general amnesty issued the previous November.

Bonney kept his promise to Wallace and testified against Dolan, Evans and Campbell in the murder of Huston Chapman. Evans and Campbell were still at large, but Dolan was bound over for trial and granted a change of venue to neighboring Doña Ana County on the grounds he could not get a fair trial in Lincoln. Judge Bristol granted the same change of venue to most of the other Dolan men bound over for trial.

With his promise to testify against Dolan fulfilled, Billy expected his own hearing on charges in the murder of Sheriff James Brady to be handled as a simple formality with the district attorney declining to prosecute, as promised by Governor Wallace. But District Attorney William Rynerson, an imposing figure at nearly seven feet tall, was no friend of Wallace's and refused to go along with the deal. Rynerson owed his appointment as district attorney to Wallace's predecessor, Samuel B. Axtell, and was an unabashed friend of Dolan. [196]

Billy was left stranded that day in Judge Bristol's courtroom. His promised benefactor, Wallace, had departed Lincoln for Santa Fe soon after the grand jury handed up its indictments. The governor said he had to prepare to testify in the upcoming military court of inquiry of Colonel Dudley, accused of being a party to the murder of Alexander McSween, the burning of his home and the looting of the Tunstall store.

Forced to fend for himself, the Kid was no courtroom match for the towering Rynerson. The district attorney was hell-bent on prosecuting the young outlaw to the fullest extent, including putting a noose around Billy's skinny neck. Judge Bristol upheld Rynerson's arguments throughout and bound Billy over for a July trial in Doña Ana County, which, unlike Lincoln County, harbored very few friends of Billy the Kid. Billy had no choice but to cling to a dimming hope that Wallace would uphold his end of their amnesty deal and come through for him when he faced trial.

Within days after Judge Bristol gaveled an end to his court, a military court of inquiry into the case of Colonel Dudley convened on May 9 at Fort Stanton. Its purpose was to determine if sufficient grounds existed for ordering a court martial for Dudley.

Governor Wallace, just in from Santa Fe, was the first witness to testify in the proceedings. He stated that Dudley was so feared and intimidating that the people in Lincoln refused to sign affidavits against murderers who were known friends of the colonel. It was damning testimony, indeed, but defense lawyer Henry Waldo, a former chief justice, skillfully drew from Wallace an admission he did not know of these intimidations firsthand but gathered the complaints from folks after coming to Lincoln.

The court declared his testimony hearsay and disregarded it.

After his faltering performance under Waldo's piercing cross-examination, the governor was excused and returned to Santa Fe while the inquiry proceeded for another six weeks. During that time, Juan Patrón, among a dozen others, including Billy the Kid and the prosecutor's star witness Susan McSween, took the stand against Dudley.

Patrón substantiated Wallace's claims of Dudley's use of intimidation to subvert affidavits against his friends.

When the inquiry turned its attention to charges that Dudley ordered soldiers to prevent the rescue of those in the burning McSween house, Billy was brought before the court to testify. Under oath, Billy swore that he and Jose Chaves y Chaves, in their dash for safety, were shot at by three soldiers while fleeing the burning house that evening of July 19, 1878.

The case against Dudley unraveled quickly with the erratic testimony of Susan McSween, the colonel's primary accuser. Her behavior on the stand swung from being demurely hesitant to acidly querulous at times. At one point, she blithely admitted she could not remember the contents of her affidavit accusing Dudley of her husband's murder—perhaps the most damning admission of all. Under Waldo's pressing cross-examination, she said little, if anything, to damage Dudley's case or advance her own. On July 18, the officers of the court found in favor of Dudley and declared that a court martial was not necessary.

After testifying, Billy was returned to house arrest in Patrón's store. By then, he had lost all trust in Wallace. Ignoring Billy's letters for help, the governor offered no signs he would rescue Billy from his July murder trial. On June 17, an angry and frustrated Billy Bonney walked out of Patrón's store and declared himself free. Billy, Folliard and Scurlock reined their horses northward and rode unhindered up the draws of the Capitan Mountains toward their old stomping grounds around Fort Sumner.

By his own thinking, Billy had tried to stay within the law for two years. His efforts produced nothing but broken promises. As Tunstall's hired hand, he had been promised a ranch. While defending the McSweens with his life, he was promised pay he never received. And now, Wallace's promise of amnesty in exchange for Billy's testimony proved to be a sham. Billy the Kid resumed doing what he knew best—taking without paying.

More than a year later, Patrón submitted his affidavit to the county government for housing and feeding Bonney and his pals. He charged five dollars as rent for keeping the prisoners and one dollar a day for feeding each of them. The bill totaled one hundred and nine dollars.[197]

Lincoln N. Mex,
November 12th 1880

Lincoln County
In a/c with
Juan B. Patron   Dr.

Rent of House for Keeping Prisoners
from March 21st/79 to June 17th/79
@ $5.00 per month $14. 33
To Board of Wm Bonny   27 days   27. 00
"   "   " Lucas Gallegos 27 days   27. 00
"   "   " Dock Scurlock 27 days   27. 00
"   "   " Thomas O'Folliard 10 days 10. 00
"   "   " Dan Dedrick 4 days   4. 00

                    Total $109.33

Territory of New Mexico }
County of Lincoln   }

Juan B. Patron, being duly sworn deposes and says; that the forgoing account is just and correct, and that the County of Lincoln is justly indebted to deponent in the above a/c.

Juan B. Patron

Sworn to and subscribed this 13th day of November A.D. 1880.

Ben N. Ellis,
Probate Clerk
By S. R. Corbeth
Dpty

Juan Patrón's affidavit for boarding Billy the Kid and his pals.

Despite Wallace's six-week stay in Lincoln, he had little to show for his efforts. Jesse Evans and Billy Campbell were still at large. Colonel Dudley escaped a career-ending court martial. Billy the Kid, as a wanted murderer, was free again, rustling stock and dealing cards in the saloons around Fort Sumner and Puerto de Luna.

Billy and Folliard soon teamed up with Charlie Bowdre and Doc Scurlock and began a spree of cattle rustling. In one raid, they drove off one hundred head of cattle on John Chisum's range, rebranded them at the ranch where Bowdre and Scurlock worked, and sold them for ten dollars a head. Their easy profits kept Billy and his boys living in high style.

If there was a single success Wallace pointed to, it was the "most excellent" work of Captain Juan Patrón and The Lincoln County Rifles, which he praised in his report to the legislature, requesting funds to pay the militiamen for their services. The militia, he said, provided an efficient posse for the county sheriff and lifted local morale. "It was [as] perfect as in any community in this country," Wallace boasted.[198]

The governor explained to the legislators that he turned to the use of a militia because terrorism was so widespread in Lincoln County that peopled "lived in constant fear" and that civil authorities "found it impossible to perform the functions of their offices." He reminded them that President Hayes had declared the county in a "state of insurrection."

Praising Patrón's leadership in keeping the riflemen on constant patrols, Wallace said the militia rendered "great service" and its members should be compensated. During deployments, Patrón and his men rounded up most of the two hundred men later indicted by the grand jury. In its third deployment alone, Wallace pointed out, a detachment returned with "fifteen prisoners in custody, some of them very desperate characters." They included Marion Turner and John Jones, both wanted in the murder of Alexander McSween.

As reported by *Thirty Four*, a weekly newspaper in Mesilla, most of those indicted "plead the governor's pardon and were discharged" under Wallace's general amnesty issued on November 13, 1878. Nevertheless, Wallace convinced himself that general amnesty had a salutary effect in restoring peace in Lincoln, claiming that only one murder—that of Huston Chapman—had occurred in the county since the amnesty was issued. He later declared in a letter to Secretary of Interior Schurz that the amnesty brought closure to Lincoln's "murderous past" and that the Dolan and McSween factions "are dead as organizations."[199]

Wallace dissolved The Lincoln County Rifles on July 15, 1879. During its nearly four-month existence, some militiamen spent as many as twenty-seven days on patrol and others as few as two days, at a pay rate of fifty cents a day. As their leader, Patrón was salaried at fifty dollars a month.

In early 1880, the legislature appropriated twenty-two hundred dollars to cover the militia's expenses. Of that amount, one thousand dollars went to the militiamen and nearly two hundred and fifty dollars to Patrón. Jose Montano received five hundred and sixty dollars and Isaac Ellis one hundred and forty dollars for supplies. Ellis also was reimbursed fourteen dollars for clean underwear and a burial suit for an outlaw killed by the riflemen.[200]

While on patrol, Patrón kept his militiamen and their animals well fed. Montano and Ellis supplied the company with hundreds of pounds of corn, rice and flour, several slaughtered sheep and more than two hundred and fifty cartridges. Their invoices revealed a chilling irony. It was more expensive to keep Patrón's men in coffee than it was to send a man to an early grave. A pound of coffee cost thirty-three cents. A single bullet cost four cents. [201]

CHAPTER 17

Married Life Amidst Thieves

━━━◆◆╳◆◆━━━

When Juan Patrón met Tranquilino Labadie at St. Michael's College, he made a friend for life. Their kinship became so strong they considered themselves brothers and swore an unflagging loyalty to each other. During weekend breaks at school, they often relaxed at Labadie's family home in Puerto de Luna, near Santa Rosa. There, Juan met Tranquilino's younger sister, Beatriz. Admiring her good looks, poise and intelligence, he always welcomed opportunities to talk to her.

In mid-1879, Patrón found himself at a major crossroads in life, pondering the possibility of marriage and where to settle. After his militia brought to justice many of the rustlers and murderers plaguing Lincoln County that spring, the area slowly gained stability and order. Crime and violence, while still common, surrendered gradually to effective sheriffs and judges now untethered to partisan bosses. And the men who once employed every devious and lethal means to eliminate their enemies in years past strived to recast themselves as reputable citizens.

None craved respectability more than the cunning Jimmy Dolan. Ever resourceful, the archenemy of John Tunstall had climbed from the wreckage of war and bankruptcy to regain a new eminence in Lincoln, posing a huge worry for Patrón. So long as Dolan tried to suppress or rationalize his crooked, immoral methods of the past, Patrón envisioned a target permanently sewn to his coat. To preserve his own life, he decided to leave Lincoln for good.

In fleeing Lincoln, Patrón left behind a distinguished political career, a reputation of unblemished integrity and the inchoate adobe walls of a church he had vowed to build when first coming to Lincoln nine years earlier. In April 1876, Patrón had teamed with Padre Sambrano Tafoya, the newly assigned priest to Lincoln, in a campaign to raise money among local Catholics to build a new church on Lincoln's main street.[202]

The *Weekly New Mexican* predicted the church would be built by year's end, but the project quickly became mired in disputes over ownership of the church site and murky property titles, a frequent occurrence in Lincoln at the time. In 1877, a site finally was acquired. It sat adjacent to the underground jail being built then with adobes supplied by Patrón for the jailer's house above the jail pit. Both sites sat across the street from Patrón's home and place of business. As the walls of the church slowly began their climb, one adobe upon another, work came to an abrupt halt, due to violent spasms in Lincoln, disrupting life for the next two years. Work on the church never resumed, and Patrón's departure sadly sounded the death knell for the church he always wanted in Lincoln.[203]

At Tranquilino Labadie's insistence, Patrón took temporary refuge at the Labadie family's ranch home near Santa Rosa. As days turned into weeks with the Labadies, Patrón's admiration for Beatriz Labadie slowly evolved into romantic feelings for her. At twenty-one, she was six years younger than Patrón, well educated and ready for marriage. She also was well acquainted with her suitor's respected standing in the Hispanic community and his accomplishments in public life.

Tranquilino Labadie in 1912

Patrón eventually asked Lorenzo Labadie and his wife Rallitos Gutierrez for their daughter's hand in marriage. They happily acceded to his wish. Patrón's penchant for politics endeared him to the Labadies, for deeply embedded in their gene pool was a strong commitment to public service, beginning with the family patriarch. Lorenzo Labadie had served his country for a half century before turning to ranching in Puerto de Luna.

Unbeknownst to Patrón, his future bride had been previously promised in marriage to Amado Chaves on the day of her baptism. Young Chaves was five years old at the time, the son of Beatriz's older sister, Dolores. In those days, boys and girls had little say about whom they would marry. Their parents, more often the mothers, made the matches without consulting their children. And it was not uncommon for close relatives to marry, even among first cousins, so as not to mix blood outside the family.

Chaves, who became New Mexico's first superintendent of public instruction in 1851 and later the mayor of Santa Fe, described the matchmaking in a letter he penned in 1927 to a young acquaintance, Laurence F. Lee. The moment of his betrothal occurred just hours after Beatriz was baptized and her family had returned home from church.

"Aunt Rallitos placed her in my mother's lap," Chaves wrote, "and my aunt announced: 'Here my dear sister, you have Amado's bride.' My mother replied: 'I accept her with all my heart.' As we grew up, Beatriz and I considered ourselves engaged. If I had not gone to Washington, D. C., for an education, we surely would have been married. But in the interval she found someone else."[204]

That someone was Juan Patrón, whom the Labadies happily welcomed into their family. In late 1879, Juan and Beatriz were married in the town of Anton Chico, a *placita* or small settlement twenty-five miles northwest of Santa Rosa.

Threats on Patrón's life had not abated since he joined the Labadie family. "On several occasions," his daughter Rayitos wrote later, "bands of men came to Santa Rosa in search of my father. He was eager to go out and face these hostile men; however, the Labadies feared for his life and pleaded with him on such occasions to remain inside."[205]

The Lincoln County gang's persistent attempts to goad Patrón into facing them became too unsettling for the Labadies. Lorenzo Labadie's wife, Rallitos, suggested that everyone would be safer if the newly wedded Patróns moved to another location, where they would be free of taunts by the murderous men of Lincoln County. All agreed and the Patróns began planning their move to Puerto de Luna.

Days later, with his wife Beatriz riding beside him on a loaded surrey, Patrón drove his team of horses to Puerto de Luna, a small settlement of sheep ranches and orchards about ten miles southeast of Santa Rosa. They settled temporarily into an old house described by one citizen as "primitive living quarters," a stark contrast from the spacious, comfortable Labadie ranch home they had just left.[206]

Beatriz Labadie and Juan Patrón in 1879

When Patrón left Lincoln with its unfinished church, his fervor for church building accompanied him to Puerto de Luna, where Catholics had only a small mission chapel in which to worship. Their pastor was Padre Auguste Francois Joseph Redon, who oversaw a flock of fifteen hundred Catholics scattered throughout Guadalupe County.

Patrón soon teamed with Padre Redon in organizing a local campaign to erect a church. It was a simple partnership. The priest would solicit financial help from among the faithful, and his merchant friend would encourage contributions from local businessmen. Their lofty ambition was to "prepare a temple which in a time not too distant will become a parish seat," Padre Redon stated in *La Revista Catolica*, the diocesan newspaper. The padre set a goal of twelve hundred dollars in collections. The solicitation proved successful. Melqulades Ramirez donated the church site, and construction began soon afterwards.[207]

Patrón liked his business prospects in Puerto de Luna. It was a thriving village on the Pecos River and the government seat of a county that was growing. However, it also was gaining a reputation as "a thieves nest," often visited by Billy Bonney and his gang and roving bands of cattle thieves up from old Mexico. Whether Billy and Patrón ever encountered each other again after Billy fled Patrón's custody in Lincoln is unknown.[208]

One of Billy's favorite Puerto de Luna haunts was the combined home and store owned by a Polish immigrant, Alexander Grzelachowski. Known as a scholar and linguist, Grzelachowski had been a Catholic priest before settling in Puerto de Luna in the 1870s as a rancher and merchant. Locals affectionately called the jolly fellow Padre Polaco. To Puerto de Luna natives, Billy was known fondly as "Billito," especially by the young senoritas he often escorted onto the dance floor to fast-step the fandango at *bailes* Padre Polaco hosted in his home.[209]

It was not by his choosing that Billy would eat his last Christmas dinner in leg irons at Padre Polaco's home in 1880. Two days before, Billy and three other outlaws had been captured by Deputy Sheriff Pat Garrett at an abandoned adobe-rock house in Stinking Springs, a barren sheep camp about thirty miles to the south. Garrett and his posse of mostly Texas cowboys had surrounded the small house, trapping Billy and the others inside without food for nearly a day. After his best friend Charlie Bowdre was fatally wounded in a valiant but futile attempt at escaping, a cocky, disgusted and hungry Billy the Kid surrendered, sauntering outside to face the towering six-foot-four-inch tall Garrett.

The food the Garrett entourage ate that snowy Christmas Day at Padre Polaco's table may have been nothing more than regular fare. Almost certainly, it was not a feast of wild turkey as some authors romanticized in writing about Billy the Kid. More likely, it was a traditional Hispanic meal, much like the one the Labadie and Patrón families shared that Christmas afternoon at Lorenzo Labadie's ranch house, a few miles away.

Sheriff Pat Garret in 1881

A great grandson to Padre Polaco, Daniel Flores, writes in his history, *Puerto de Luna*, that the meal served to the Garrett party may well have consisted of mere leftovers from the Grezalachowski family's own noon meal since the group arrived about 2 p.m. Flores suggests that the meal probably was like any other the family ate on a daily basis.

"It may have included mutton from one of Don Alejandro's large flocks of sheep," Flores said. "Potatoes and chili may also have been on the menu or perhaps a pot of pinto beans with salted pork.... For [dessert], they may have eaten some *empanadas* [meat or fruit turnovers]."[210]

Christmas Day was celebrated differently in 1880 than today, Flores said, noting that Garrett was on the job that day transporting his four prisoners to Las Vegas. "And Don Alejandro did not even close his store," Flores added. "For him, Christmas Day was business as usual."

Before reaching Puerto de Luna, the Garrett posse and their prisoners stopped on Christmas Eve at Fort Sumner, about twenty-five miles to the south on the Pecos. Billy and Dave Rudabaugh were deemed the most dangerous of the four prisoners and were fitted for leg irons. Because the blacksmith lacked enough material to make leg irons for Billy Wilson and Tom Pickett, Garrett said they would be put into irons later.

Now shackled together, Billy and Rudabaugh were led by two of

Garrett's men tó a two-story building that was once the officers' quarters at the former army post and now served as the family home of Pete Maxwell. Pete's father had purchased Fort Sumner from the government two years after the post was closed down in 1868.

Maxwell's mother, Luz Beaubien Maxwell, had asked Garrett earlier if he would allow Billy and her sixteen-year-old daughter, Paulita, to say their good-byes. Garrett politely consented but insisted that the Kid remain in irons. It was well known around Fort Sumner that Billy was quite a ladies man, and the attractive Paulita was believed to be his favorite among the girls he wooed there.

After Billy and Rudabaugh were brought inside the Maxwell house by their guards, Jim East and Lee Hall, Paulita's mother asked if Billy could be unshackled and allowed to meet with her daughter in another room. "Of course, we had to refuse, although all the world loves a lover." Jim East wrote later. "The lovers embraced and she gave Billy one of those soul kisses the novelists tell us about."[211]

After a few moments, the two lovers were pulled apart, and Billy and Rudabaugh were led back to Garrett. Billy and Rudabaugh were helped onto a two-mule wagon, while Garret and his men saddled up for the long, bitter cold ride to Puerto de Luna before moving on to Las Vegas.

Before his capture, Billy made his home in Fort Sumner, according to the 1880 census recorded that June. Lorenzo Labadie was the official census taker who sat down with the Kid. Billy gave his name as William Bonney and told Labadie he shared a home with his longtime sidekick, Charlie Bowdre, and his wife, Manuela. Citizens around Fort Sumner, however, wondered if the two boys shared more than just a house.[212]

Bonney told Labadie he was twenty-five years old at the time, and Labadie recorded that Bonney and Bowdre both "work in cattle." If the word "work" implied they came by their own stock honesty, it was a total fabrication. As accomplished cattle thieves, their "work" consisted mainly of separating honest ranchers from their cattle. Throughout his short life, Billy never could settle on his true age or place of birth. When he talked to Labadie, he was more nearly twenty years old.

That summer, a traveling photographer came to Fort Sumner and offered to take tintype portraits of local individuals for only a few cents apiece. The cameraman's offer drew settlers from miles around, and Billy was among those who decided to have his picture taken. It is the only picture of Billy the Kid that exists today.

The surviving photograph is hardly flattering. Dressed in rumpled, trail-worn clothes with a lopsided felt hat atop his head, Billy is captured with his mouth partially agape, exposing his buckteeth, and his eyelids drooping over tired eyes. It is in sharp contrast to the neat, well-dressed Billy reportedly seen around Fort Sumner, especially if he was going to a dance, according to Paulita Maxwell.

In the photograph, a cartridge belt is wrapped around his waist with a six-shooter stuffed into a hanging holster on his right side. His trusty 1873 Model Winchester rifle is in the grasp of his left hand with its butt resting on the floor. These were the tools of a rustler's trade. When free, Billy and his tools were inseparable.

CHAPTER 18

Labadie Connection

———◈◈◈◈◈———

W hen Juan Patrón ended his long bachelorhood, his marriage to Beatriz landed him in one of the most respected and deeply rooted families of New Mexico. Known as "a tough little frontiersman," Lorenzo Labadie had survived many years of danger and adventure in service to his country. His life story unfolds like a collection of anecdotal vignettes.

During a span of fifty years, he wore the sheriff badges of three New Mexico counties, served eight years as U.S. Indian Agent to the Mescalero Apaches, helped to settle them onto the controversial Bosque Redondo Reservation and rode alongside the legendary Colonel Christopher "Kit" Carson in pursuit of renegade Indians found plundering white settlements in New Mexico.

Labadie was born in Tome, a small village on the Rio Grande River near Belen. His family name stems from French ancestry. Dominic Labadie, his great grandfather, had come to America from France, first settling in St. Louis and finally in Santa Fe in 1765. As a medical doctor, the twenty-seven-year-old Frenchman prospered and within a year took a wife, marrying Maria Micaela Padilla, daughter of one of the original founding families of Albuquerque. Like most Frenchmen who married New Mexican native women, Dominic chose to immerse himself in the Spanish culture and community, even to the degree of being called Domingo. He and Micaela eventually had fifteen children. Among their five sons was Juan Pablo Labadie, who later would marry Maria Rosa de los Reyes Cisneros. The newlyweds made their home in Tome, where their son Jose Lorenzo Labadie was born on August 10, 1823.

Because Tome was a frequent target of Apache and Navajo raiders, Lorenzo learned as a teenager to defend himself against attacking Indians. By the time he matured into his early twenties, Lorenzo had earned a reputation as a skillful and fearless scout. Military expeditions on the hunt for bands of marauding Indians often hired him for his tracking skills.

In the summer of 1857, Colonel William W. Loring hired Lorenzo to help his soldiers track down Chief Cuchillo Negro and his band of Mescalero Apaches. The Indians had been terrorizing white settlements along the Rio Grande, stretching from Socorro in the north to El Paso on the Mexican border. Labadie led the soldiers to the Indians' encampment in a deep canyon near Truth or Consequences. A fierce battle erupted, lasting several hours, as Labadie and his soldiers met deadly incoming arrows with their own rifle fire. Chief Negro was killed and his warriors were sent scampering in retreat. Labadie and the troopers returned home unscathed.[213]

Lorenzo Labadie (seated) and Cresenciano Gallegos in 1880

At age twenty-nine, Lorenzo decided he was ready for marriage. It came late in life for a frontiersman, but on February 16, 1852, Labadie and Maria "Rallitas" de los Reyes Refugio Gutierrez were married in the Church of St. Francis in Santa Fe. As fate would have it, nine days after Lorenzo's wedding, Juan Patrón, at five days old, was christened at the same altar and eventually would become Labadie's son-in-law.[214]

Rallitas had been raised and educated by a great aunt, Maria Gertrudis Barcelo, better known as Madame La Tules, an intriguing woman who dominated society in mid-nineteenth-century Santa Fe. To writers who have tried to chronicle her life, she remains an enigmatic character. She has been given varied and conflicting descriptions, ranging from "fecund young woman of incredible beauty" to "common prostitute," "supreme queen of refinement and fashion," and "respectable woman and faithful wife."[215]

Whatever she may have been, no one questions that she was the best professional gambler in all of the New Mexico territory. In 1835, La Tules and her husband Manuel Antonio Sisneros, a member of a long-established New Mexican family, settled in Santa Fe. There, she opened up the most glittering gambling salon in the territory, covering an entire block along Burro Alley between Palace and San Francisco streets. Its lavish card rooms attracted gamblers ranging from grizzled old miners to elite businessmen. Madame La Tules's patrons came from all over the country to challenge her at monte, a game of pure chance won by matching cards from the deal to cards placed face up in the center of the table. It was the most popular gambling game in the territory, and no one was better at dealing monte than Madame La Tules.

While dealing, she wore a common, loose-fitting dress like Mexican peasant women and no jewelry, portraying herself as just a simple country girl, trying to win at a man's game. It was clever masking of her deftness as a wily monte dealer and usually disarmed her challengers. But in social circles, the gaming madam presented herself in sartorial splendor. She tucked herself into tight-fitting silk bodices set off with a blaze of rings bearing precious stones. Heavy gold chains hung from her neck, including one with a solid gold crucifix.

Years later, Rallitas Labadie came into Madam La Tules's life. She was the infant daughter of the lady gambler's niece, Raphaela, whom La Tules adopted in the 1830s. When La Tules died in 1852, her will provided for her niece and daughter Rallitas. The celebrated woman also left behind a legacy as one of the most enigmatic characters of the Western frontier.[216]

Rallitas and Lorenzo Labadie were married one month after La Tules's death. The previous year, Lorenzo had pinned on his first sheriff's badge in Valencia County, where he soon made history overseeing the first legal hanging in New Mexico on May 25, 1852. Several years later, Lorenzo moved his family into Santa Fe County, where he served three terms as sheriff before taking his last job as sheriff in Las Vegas as the top lawman in San Miguel County. His experience there would prove valuable years later when a murder occurred in the dining room of the St. Nicholas Hotel on March 2, 1880. The *Las Vegas Gazette* reported the incident in the grand style of opera boffo:[217]

> James Moorhead, representing the wholesale liquor house of Derby and Day, St. Louis, was shot at about ten this morning by James Allen, a waiter of the St. Nicholas Hotel. Moorhead called for eggs, and the waiter said that the cook hadn't time to serve them.
>
> A quarrel began, they clinched and were parted. Allen went back into the dining room, got a pistol and rushed into the office where Moorhead was standing. He aimed the pistol at the salesman's head and said: "Get down on your knees and ask my pardon." In attempting to take the pistol from him, Moorhead was shot, the ball entering the left side, passing through the stomach and coming out at the right side over the liver.
>
> When Allen, 20, was arrested by an officer, he was found in the dining-room, quietly preparing the table for dinner. Moorhead lies in a critical condition and is expected to die tonight. Great excitement prevails and it is rumored that Allen will be lynched tonight.

As predicted, Moorhead died at about 10 o'clock that night. A few days later, the same paper reported that the jail was under threat of attack by a mob bent on hanging Allen, only to be held at bay by a force of twenty deputies. Allen's lawyer quickly won a change of venue to protect his client, and the judge directed that the prisoner be transferred immediately to the custody of the sheriff of Santa Fe to prevent a lynching. Local authorities summoned three well-known citizens for help. They appointed Lorenzo Labadie, his new son-in-law Juan Patrón, and Pablo Anaya as a special posse to provide Allen's safe transfer.

The newspaper continued its report on the unfolding drama:

At exactly the regular time for the train's arrival, the prisoner was quietly carried to the depot in a carriage without attracting any observation. Here a difficulty occurred as it was found that the train would be three hours late. It was impossible to take Allen into the depot without his presence being known and thus rousing the unruly element of the town. To take him back to jail was also quite sure to attract attention. The night was too cold for him to remain out doors, as he had no overcoat, although he himself, in his anxiety to be taken beyond the reach of mob violence, was willing to endure the cold.

Finally, he was conveyed to the house of a person who could be trusted and there kept until nearly 4 o'clock when the train arrived and was then swiftly conveyed on board. Allen arrived safely in Santa Fe yesterday morning before the people of East Las Vegas knew that he has been removed.

The special posse succeeded in its stealthy mission that day, only to learn later in the pages of the *Gazette* that "there appears to be no record to show that the waiter was brought to trial," thus ending the tale of the hotel guest who wanted eggs for breakfast but got lead instead.

Like his friend Kit Carson, Labadie was a sympathetic and loyal friend to many of the Native Americans and a fearsome foe to others. This rare combination singled him out for appointment as U.S. Indian Agent to the Mescalero Apaches during the early months of the Civil War. Early in his new job, Labadie was in Las Cruces on government business when a Confederate army from El Paso took over the town. Because his loyalty to the Union was well known, local Confederate sympathizers wanted to tar and feather the agent. But word reached Labadie before the plan could be hatched, and he skipped town just in time to avoid the pain and humiliation.[218]

Labadie had a second run-in with Confederate troops when one hundred of them from Texas overran Fort Stanton near Lincoln in August 1861 and occupied it. While attending to Indian business there, Labadie and Bonifacio Chaves were taken prisoners by the Texans and held for four days. But political connections saved them. They were released after the Texas commander learned that Chaves was the stepson of New Mexico's incoming governor, Henry Connelly.

After the war, Labadie was asked by the U.S. government to carry out his most dangerous mission as Indian agent. He was directed to ride into the high plains of Texas, seek out the Comanche and Kiowa, and convince them to cease their raids and release all of their white captives.

Showing no fear, Labadie rose to the challenge and, with only six companions, spurred the horses eastward to the Texas panhandle. As they approached the Texas border, he scattered his men in all directions to find the Indians and call them to a special powwow. While the hunt was on, Labadie arranged for more than seven hundred teepees to be set up at the planned meeting site.

His audacity astounded the fierce Comanche and Kiowa, both stunned that a white man would venture into their lands and demand they make peace. By whatever persuasive powers Labadie used, the Indians listened to his proposal and agreed to his terms. When the Indians' top chiefs returned from raids in Mexico, the tribes released their captives and stopped their attacks on settlements in New Mexico and Texas. Later, Labadie wrote in his official report that "these Indians are of good heart and desire to live at peace with our government."[219]

When Labadie accepted his appointment in 1861 as Indian agent to the Mescalero Apaches, the job paid three thousand dollars a year. For that salary, he would enter the most dangerous and tumultuous period of his long life. At age thirty-nine, Labadie was an energetic man of tremendous tenacity and yet deeply sympathetic to the wronged and disinherited. Because of Labadie's courage and compassion, his superiors chose him for the daunting task of convincing the Mescaleros to lay down their arms and move onto a future reservation.

Labadie's first official report on September 25, 1862 was less than hopeful as the Mescaleros continued their attacks on settlers during his first year as agent. He wrote that in the previous month, the Indians "killed some forty men and six children, and carried a number of children into captivity, some of whom, after keeping them in the mountains for several days, were stripped and turned loose.... The property robbed consisted of horses, mules, donkeys and cattle."[220]

A firm hand was needed to reduce the Indian raids reported by Labadie, and the army chose General James Henry Carleton for the job, making him the absolute ruler over law and order in New Mexico. At age forty-eight, Carlton was a battle-hardened and aggressive officer who demanded strict discipline. He also harbored a stubborn streak and could not admit an error or take a backward step when required. Unable to pause and change course when handling Indians, he plunged straight into a disaster, involving not only himself but Labadie, Carson and practically all of the New Mexico Indians.

Carleton decided that the Mescaleros were to be humbled first, then the Navajo. He persuaded a reluctant Colonel Kit Carson to take charge of the army troops in the field and, with his own New Mexico militiamen, lead the attack on the Mescaleros. Foreseeing an unnecessary slaughtering of Indians, Carson refused but eventually yielded to Carleton's pressure. Labadie was directed to accompany Carson's expedition but instructed *not* to propose or accept offers of peace until the Mescaleros were properly punished in accordance with Carleton's orders.

The savageness of Carleton's final instruction to Carson shocked him and Labadie. "All Indian men of that tribe are to be killed whenever and wherever you can find them," the general ordered. "You have been sent to punish them for their treachery and crimes. If they beg for peace, their chiefs and twenty of their principal men must come to Santa Fe to have a talk there."[221]

Carleton's surrender-or-be-killed ultimatum to the Mescaleros came to a climax in the last days of October when Captain James Graydon led a scouting party out of newly occupied Fort Stanton. He came upon a band of Mescaleros led by the aged Chief Manuelito. Seeing the mounted troopers approaching, Manuelito raised his hand, signifying he wanted to talk peace. Captain Graydon, blindly obeying Carleton's standing order, fired into the band without warning, killing Manuelito, his deputy chief, Jose Largo, nine other warriors and one woman.

Carson and Labadie were outraged over Graydon's cold-blooded murder of the Indians in the face of a gesture of peace, for they had learned that Manuelito was on his way to Santa Fe to ask for peace. By early November, the hunted Mescaleros were weakened by hunger, out-gunned, and ready for peace.

In a final confrontation with army troops, an encampment of five hundred Mescaleros chose to run rather than fight. Those who survived hiked across the ranges to Fort Stanton and asked their trusted friend Kit Carson for protection. Told they wanted to talk peace, Carson sent five of their leaders to Santa Fe to face General Carleton, accompanied by their agent Lorenzo Labadie and a military escort.

Vanquished in battle but not in spirit, the five Indians stood before the conquering American general as Chief Cadette served as their spokesman. His words were translated by Labadie:

You are stronger than we. We have fought you as long as we had rifles and powder; but your weapons are better than ours. Give us weapons and turn us loose, and we will fight you again; but we are worn out; we have no more heart; we have no provisions, no means to live; your troops are everywhere; our springs and waterholes are either occupied or overlooked by your young men. You have driven us from our last and best stronghold, and we have no more heart. Do with us as may seem good to you, but do not forget we are men and braves.[222]

A stoic Carleton sat unmoved by Cadette's words. His eyes locked onto the faces of the five Indians, the general sternly responded that they had only one choice if they wanted to live: all Mescaleros who wanted to cooperate were to go to a new army post called Fort Sumner under development near one of the Apaches' favorite camping areas known as the Bosque Redondo. Carleton said they would be fed there if they remained orderly, and when all of the Mescaleros were settled at the Bosque reservation, he would be willing to discuss a treaty of peace.

Labadie also favored a reservation system. "The only permanent remedy...is in the colonization of these Indians," he wrote in his 1862 report. "The Mescalero Apaches have the best lands and, with the aid of the government, they can soon be made to raise grain and vegetables enough for their support." He said the Navajos also should be confined to "agricultural districts," but separate from the Mescaleros, because the two tribes were mortal enemies.

The first of the Mescaleros began gathering at Fort Sumner in early 1863. By March, about four hundred men, women and children were being fed there. By midsummer, most of the Mescaleros were living on the Bosque Redondo.

Under Labadie's watchful eye, the Indians, working side-by-side with soldiers, dammed the Pecos to irrigate crops, planted trees and even built a slaughterhouse. The Mescaleros proved more fortunate with their gardens than raising corn. They had ninety-four gardens spread over one hundred acres, growing melons, pumpkins, chili peppers, green beans, fruits and some tobacco. In their first year, they sold four thousand dollars worth of garden products to the army.

The Apaches also proved to be steadfast warriors for their agent. Labadie reported on two battles with the Navajo in which the Apaches distinguished themselves. In one, he and twenty Apaches overtook a war party of one hundred and thirty Navajo herding one thousand stolen sheep. After a four-hour fight, Labadie and his warriors succeeded in retaking the stolen stock and killing twelve Navajos while losing only one Apache. Two weeks later, the Navajos returned to Fort Sumner and drove off sixty horses belonging to the Apaches. Labadie and sixty of his warriors, accompanied by a Catholic priest and fifteen mounted soldiers, tracked down the Navajos, engaged them in a seven-hour battle and recovered most of the horses. "The Mescaleros are very prompt to serve the government and when thus employed are cheerful and obedient as regular soldiers," Labadie later wrote in his report. [223]

Writing his army superiors about the December firefight with the Navajos, General Carleton expressed high praise on the gallantry of the Apaches, Labadie and Father Fialon, the chaplain at Fort Stanton. "It was a handsome little battle on the open plains," he wrote. "The Apache Chiefs Cadette and Blanco were very distinguished." In a rare expression of praise toward the Indians, Carleton asked for permission to issue a suit of clothes to each Apache who took part in the fight. "The government should give them some token of appreciation of such fidelity and gallantry," he exhorted.[224]

From the very beginning of General Carleton's colonization of the Bosque Redondo as an Indian reservation, Lorenzo Labadie and Dr. Michael Steck, superintendent of Indian Affairs in New Mexico, strenuously opposed the settling of the Navajo there to live with the Mescalaros. Labadie called it a "fatal error," because the two tribes harbored a "deadly hatred" for each other. Steck called the pairing of the tribes "impractical," because the reservation lacked sufficient land to support three thousand Apaches and potentially another fifteen thousand Navajo. Brushing aside their objections like dusting off shoulder dandruff, an implacable Carleton pressed on with his doomed plan.[225]

From the first days that the Navajo came to the Bosque, their animosity toward the Apaches showed. The Navajo began tilling ground belonging to the Apaches, and when the crops ripened, the Navajo stole what the Apaches planted. Whenever they could, the Apaches fought the Navajo with a vengeance. Unfortunately, Labadie's prediction of promised fighting between the two tribes proved true.

As the tribal conflicts continued, Carleton and Labadie remained at loggerheads over the issue of keeping the Navajo on the reservation. Supporting Labadie's position, Dr. Steck suggested to his Washington superiors that the Navajo be allowed to go back to their own country so tranquility could return to the Bosque. Carleton forbade the idea. "The Navajo should never leave the Bosque and never shall, if I can prevent it," the resolute general declared in 1864.[226]

In the eyes of the general, Labadie had gone from "a good Indian agent when attending to his business" to an agitating nemesis. Soon after Labadie reported to Steck that Carleton's soldiers were feeding his Indians meat from diseased cattle that had died, Labadie found himself in hot water.

Someone concocted a dubious accusation that there was something crooked going on in supplying beef to the Indians, and supposedly it involved Labadie and a Captain Morton of the post garrison. While the story seemed absurd on the surface, a vengeful Carleton seized on it and brought Morton before a court-martial in hopes of implicating Labadie.

The military court cleared Morton, but Carleton still wanted Labadie's hide. He wrote to the adjutant general of the army that despite the court's finding he believed Labadie should be removed as Indian agent. Labadie was forced to leave the post in March 1865.[227]

Unbroken and determined to remain the Mescaleros' chief advocate, he moved the agency to his ranch a few miles north of Fort Sumner. "My departure," he wrote later, "caused great excitement and sorrow among the Navajos and Apaches, both tribes having placed in me from the beginning the love, confidence and respect that an agent seldom obtains among the Indians." In the following year, Labadie was cleared of any wrongdoing, and his stellar reputation remained intact.[228]

Carleton imposed leaner rations for the hungry Indians after Labadie's departure, and his grip on keeping them corralled on the reservation weakened with each passing day. Soon, the misery forced upon the Indians by Carleton became intolerable. The Apaches began planning a massive escape.

Their chiefs strategized that if all of the Apaches left at once, the whole tribe might get away. They reasoned that the soldiers couldn't chase after them if all went in different directions. On the night of November 3, 1865, every Apache able to travel arose quietly, stealthily eluded their guards and vanished. When the soldiers awoke the next morning, they found an almost empty reservation, as if the Apaches had evaporated overnight. Only nine sick and crippled Apaches remained behind. The massive escape was a major embarrassment for Carleton. Calls for his relief had begun building within the War Department and Interior Department even earlier because of his stubborn mishandling of the Indians. Finally, he was relieved of command on September 1866.

In 1868, the government saw the futility of the Bosque Redondo experiment and acknowledged Navajo sovereignty in the Treaty of 1868. The Navajos began their return home in June of that year, and the Navajo Nation remains today the largest Native American community in the United States. In the end, only one man in New Mexico could walk among the Apaches and Navajos as a trusted friend. He was Lorenzo Labadie, who left the Indian Service in 1869, frustrated that his government refused his repeated pleas for a reservation solely for *his* Apaches.

Labadie eventually moved his family to near Puerto de Luna and began a new life as a sheep rancher. In July 1876, he came to the aid of his beloved Mescaleros one more time. He notified Agent Frederick C. Godfroy that he could come and get a number of stolen Mescalero horses that Puerto de Luna residents had recovered from a gang of thieves. Godfroy sent his issue-clerk Morris J. Bernstein with four Indians to reclaim the stolen horses. In the meantime, Labadie asked all citizens to bring their horses and mules into town for inspection by Bernstein and the Indians. In the end, the Mescaleros reclaimed ten horses and another seven, to which Bernstein believed they had clear title. It was a rare moment of frontier justice rendered to the Apaches by Labadie and the citizens of Puerto de Luna.[229]

CHAPTER 19

The Death of Juan Patrón

I n time, Patrón obtained a sizable land grant and built a ranch house just outside of Puerto de Luna that he called the Agua Negra. Unlike most homesteaders, he turned away from farming and raising stock and developed a bountiful orchard on his new one hundred sixty acres.

With his entrepreneurial spirit intact, he also opened a mercantile store soon after coming to Puerto de Luna. In 1883, he expanded his business interests. Partnering with William Giddings, his wife's uncle, Patrón opened a hotel into which he relocated his store and saloon, spending most of his time operating that enterprise. Soon, the former legislator became a prosperous and highly respected businessman.

For Patrón, life in Puerto de Luna progressed smoothly. As his wealth grew, so did his family. In the winter of 1880, the Patróns were blessed with their first child, a girl they christened Maria Theresa Consuelo Rayitos. Two years later, a son was born and baptized Juan Secundino Ramon Jesus. In February of 1884, Beatriz awaited the birth of a third child. As her delivery date drew near, the Patrón family moved in with Beatriz's parents near Santa Rosa, intending to stay until mother and child were fit to return home. On March 19, Beatriz delivered a healthy new daughter. She was christened Maria Dolores Felipa after Beatriz's sister.

The day after his daughter's birth, Juan Patrón stood before his old political nemesis, former Governor Samuel B. Axtell, now cloaked in the black robe of a jurist. In 1882, President Hayes had named the once discredited governor his new Chief Justice of the New Mexico Supreme Court. As chief justice, Axtell also sat as Judge of the First District Court.

On this day, he was hearing criminal cases in Las Vegas. During the previous August, a grand jury had indicted Patrón on charges of selling liquor on Sunday, carrying a deadly weapon (a pistol) and assault in a menacing manner, charges that Patrón now had to answer to Axtell.[230]

Represented by his attorney, M. Salazar, Patrón pleaded guilty to violating the blue law prohibiting Sunday liquor sales and readily paid a two-dollar fine. Then, in a separate case, he faced a jury of twelve native New Mexicans on the two more serious charges, details of which are missing in the case files. Patrón pled not guilty to both counts, and after a brief trial, the jury delivered a verdict of not guilty. Judge Axtell awarded Patrón reimbursement of his defense costs, and Puerto de Luna's most prominent citizen walked out of the courtroom exonerated.

Three weeks after his new daughter's birth, Patrón journeyed to Puerto de Luna to look after his business interests. His older daughter, Rayitos, remembered that April 7 day vividly. "I recall clinging to him, begging to go along and then being torn from him by my grandmother," she wrote. "Then he departed in a little surrey."[231]

During that Wednesday in town, Patrón met two of his brothers-in-law. One was Roman Labadie, Beatriz's brother and youngest of the five Labadie children. With him was Cresenciano Gallegos, the husband of Beatriz's older sister Dolores. The three men agreed to meet that evening at the saloon in Governor Moore's place for a drink before returning to the Labadie ranch together.

Roman Labadie in 1912

145

At About 3:30 p.m. that day, a slightly built twenty-six-year-old Texan named Michael Erskine Maney rode into town to cash a money order for his boss, George C. Peacock, the foreman at the J. J. Cox ranch. A relative newcomer to the area, Maney had left his father's ranch in Seguin, Texas six months earlier to hire on as a cowpuncher at the Cox ranch, a big spread along the Pecos about sixty miles southeast of Puerto de Luna.[232]

Maney had been in the small village several times before, drinking and taking meals with a few of the locals, including a December visit when he had several meals at Patrón's establishment. On this day, he briefly encountered Patrón as the rangy cowhand led his horse into Governor Moore's corral for the evening. After trading friendly nods, they silently went their separate ways.

At about 5 p.m., Maney joined William Ruth for dinner at his place. Ruth shared space in an adobe that housed Moore's store and a saloon Ruth operated with William Owens. Ruth also owned the monte bank and ran the saloon's popular card gaming table. After dinner, Maney ambled over to the saloon counter for a drink as Ruth aimed for the gaming table at the opposite end of the room to begin dealing monte. A pungent haze of tobacco smoke hung over the dimly lit room. Several long-bearded farmers stood drinking at the bar. Others sat at small, scarred tables, tilting back shot glasses of Double Anchor whiskey while several men shuffled around the monte table, waiting for Ruth to open the card game.

At about 7 p.m., Patrón limped into the saloon. Slowed by a lame left leg, he weaved a pathway to the monte table and joined the gambling. But luck was no lady that night for Patrón. After losing all the money he had with him, Patrón went to the bar across the room and asked Maney to treat him to a whiskey. The cowboy obliged. Over time, Maney bought him several more drinks, each time at Patrón's request.

When Maney asked his newfound drinking partner how he fared at the card game, Patrón said he lost all he had, but if Maney would loan him a dollar, he'd try to win his money back. Without hesitation, Maney slid a silver dollar on the counter toward Patrón, and the two marched over to the monte table. After Patrón quickly lost that dollar, too, William Owens joined them, and the three men returned to the bar for a drink.

After a single round of whiskies, Owens suggested they go to Tracy's saloon inside Grzelachowski's store. "Do you want me to go with you and Juan?" asked Maney, and Owens responded, "Yes, come on." As the three trooped down the street toward Tracy's place, Owens leaned against a wobbly Patrón to keep him upright and help steady his limping stride.

It became apparent the drinks had greatly impaired Patrón's walking. Witnesses believed Patrón was drunk. When the trio reached Tracy's, they found the saloon closed because the proprietor had gone to bed early.

On their return to Moore's place, Owens held onto Patrón to keep him from falling as Maney walked ahead of them by a few steps. Suddenly and for no apparent reason, Patrón became angry that the cowboy wore a holstered Colt .44 belted around his waist. Patrón hollered out to Maney.[233]

"Hey, damn you, what are you doing with that six-shooter?" Patrón demanded. "Why do you want to be carrying it?"

"My carrying a six-shooter is nothing more than a habit," Maney responded.

"Are you carrying it for me?" Patrón barked.

"I am not carrying a six-shooter for anyone," declared the young Texan.

"Nobody but a damn coward would carry a six-shooter," exclaimed Patrón. "Damn you, I'll get my six-shooter and kill you!"

Was the whiskey fueling Patrón's bluster when he challenged Maney? Or did he truly believe this relative stranger was on a mission to kill him, even though the cowboy had treated him to drinks and showed no outward signs of hostility? Patrón had ducked two unexpected attempts on his life in Lincoln and reasonably could have had lingering paranoia from those frightening incidents.

After their verbal exchange outside, Maney quickly marched into the saloon, and Patrón turned away and limped off alone toward his store. As Maney headed for the bar, Owens warned him of Patrón's reputation for being "abusive and dangerous when drinking." At the bar, Thomas Jones, a bartender who had overheard the argument outside, asked Maney what the fracas was all about. "If he made any reply, I didn't hear it because I was busy behind the bar," Jones said.[234]

About fifteen minutes later—about 10:30 p.m.—Patrón entered the saloon with an army Remington .44 revolver stuffed deep behind his waist belt. He and Maney locked eyes but said nothing as Patrón walked to the monte table where his brother-in-law Cresenciano Gallegos was seated. Patrón rested his left hand on Gallegos's shoulder and said, "Let's go, buddy. It's time we go home. I am sleepy." As he spoke, Patrón's right hand rested on the brown walnut handle of the Remington while his eyes remained riveted on Maney, standing at the bar counter about ten feet away.[235]

"Take your hand off your six-shooter," Maney ordered Patrón, fearing he was about to draw down on him. As Patrón tightened his grip on the pistol to draw it, Maney again demanded he remove his hand from the gun. When Patrón tried to yank out his pistol, the eight-inch barrel snagged in his trousers momentarily. Then, two shots exploded almost simultaneously inside the room. The cowboy's Colt barked first and hit its mark. A bullet drilled into Patrón's chest and passed through his heart. A split second later, a ball from Patrón's firing iron whistled past Maney, slamming deep into the soft adobe wall to the right of him.[236]

The thrust of Maney's shot sent Patrón reeling. As he staggered against Gregorio Baros, his Remington accidently fired again, wounding the bystander in the arm. Patrón collapsed dead at Baros's feet. Maney triggered his gun wildly two more times. One shot blew out the only coal oil lamp lighting the saloon, plunging the room into darkness and sending customers scampering for cover outside. It was about 11 p.m.[237]

Puerto de Luna saloon in which Juan Patrón was slain in 1884.
(Photo was taken in the 1890s.)

Frightened that Patrón's friends in town may try to shoot or lynch him, Maney dashed down to the Pecos and took cover behind several huge boulders in the riverbed, four hundred yards away. With Maney nowhere in sight, calmness eventually settled among the jittery men gathered outside. Ruth, Owens, Jones and Justice of the Peace Pablo Anaya then led the way back into the saloon. When Ruth relit the room lamp, they saw Patrón's body sprawled on the floor, his pistol lying six inches from his right hand.[238]

Ruth suggested to Anaya that the crime scene remain untouched until an inquest could be held, but the justice, a longtime Patrón friend, decided to conduct an impromptu inquest then and there. Anaya knelt down to feel for Patrón's pulse. Finding none, he pronounced the town's most admired citizen dead. Anaya picked up Patrón's pistol and, without examining it, handed the warm revolver to a nearby native farmer.

At dawn the next morning, a posse of fifty armed men galloped in different directions out of town in search of the killer. After spending a shivering night crouched in the frigid waters of the Pecos, Maney threaded his way toward the ranch home of George Davidson, about five miles outside of town. As Nicholas Gregio, one of the possemen, came over the rise near Davidson's place that early morning, he spotted Maney entering the ranch house. After waiting several minutes, Gregio ventured in after him. With Davidson's cooperation, Gregio arrested Maney, who surrendered peacefully.

About mid-morning, Gregio and Davidson brought Maney back to Puerto de Luna to face a preliminary hearing before Justice Anaya. A cluster of angry citizens greeted them. "There was strong talk of lynching Maney," the Las Vegas *Daily Optic* reported, "but no demonstration was made to have 'Judge Lynch' preside at the ceremonies."[239]

The persuasive powers of calmer men, led by Patrón's father-in-law, Lorenzo Labadie, quickly dissuaded those clamoring for a lynching. A tough Indian fighter who had worn the sheriff badges of three counties in times past, Labadie reminded the crowd they had laws that would deliver justice in this case. He told them the "wanton killing" of Patrón was so evident that any jury would certainly find Maney guilty of murder.[240]

With no evidence at their disposal, Patrón sympathizers nonetheless speculated that the young Texan had been sent to kill Patrón by men who feared he knew about their criminal activities during the Lincoln County War. Collectively, Patrón loyalists characterized his killing as "an unprovoked, deliberate and well-planned murder."

At his preliminary hearing before Justice Anaya that morning, Maney steadfastly maintained that he drew on Patrón in self-defense. Asked by Anaya why he was afraid that Patrón had a pistol, Maney responded in straightforward fashion: "I was scared because he threatened to kill me. When he took his pistol out, I shot him."[241]

Two others who testified at the hearing shed little light on the shooting. A confused Gregorio Baros believed it was Maney's second or third shot that plunged a slug into his arm, although other witnesses later stated it was Patrón's accidental firing as he staggered after being shot by Maney. William Ruth testified he did not see the shooting because he was cashing a check at the monte table, adding that he didn't even know Patrón was in the saloon until he saw him falling after being shot.

When the hearing concluded about two hours after midnight, Anaya ordered Maney jailed on the charge of murder and bound over to district court for trial in August. The next day, Anaya appointed George Giddings, George V. Davidson and Nicholas Gregio to deliver Maney to the San Miguel County jail in Las Vegas. As the foursome journeyed eighty miles to Las Vegas, small knots of volunteers joined the escort along the way in tribute to Patrón. When the group trotted Maney into Las Vegas, twenty armed riders encircled the accused.[242]

After Anaya's inquest the night of the shooting, he released Patrón's body to his two brothers-in-law. Cresenciano Gallegos and Roman Labadie wrapped a coarse saddle blanket around the bloody corpse. Before placing it onto Patrón's surrey, Gallegos looked for and found where the fatal bullet burrowed into the saloon wall. Mournfully, he removed a small silver crucifix hanging from his neck and jabbed it inside the bullet hole as a simple memorial. He and his brother-in-law sadly drove off with Patrón's covered body in the little buggy, heading for the Labadie ranch a few miles away.[243]

Beatriz Patrón was asleep when they arrived. "When she looked upon her dead husband, her broken heart gave way to its feelings," the Las Vegas *Daily Optic* dramatically reported, "and the scene of sorrow can never be forgotten by those present." Married only five years before that tragic night, Beatriz now found herself an unexpected widow at twenty-five, cradling a newborn baby in her arms while her mother tended to her two other small children.[244]

Three days after his death, Juan Patrón was accorded an honor generally reserved for martyred saints. He was buried beneath the vestibule of the church he helped to build, despite a 1793 edict by the Vatican banning such tributes for laypersons.

Our Lady of Refuge church had been opened only days before but was still awaiting a roof. On the frontier, it was not uncommon for active churches to be without roofs. Hefty hewn beams for vaulted roofs were hard to find and expensive, especially for struggling new churches like Our Lady of Refuge. Parishioners today are reminded of Patrón's prominence in establishing the church. His role is noted in the church's brief historical sketch. In pointed irony and twisted history, it reads:

The first mass celebrated in Puerto de Luna was for the funeral of Don Juan Patrón, who was murdered by a Texan, an emissary of the Murphy-Dolan faction that figured prominently in the Lincoln County War. It was through Don Juan's generosity that the church had been completed, and fate had it that he [would] enter it as a corpse.[245]

Hundreds of mourners from across the territory attended the funeral, which one newspaper described as the largest ever to occur in that part of New Mexico. "Friends, acquaintances and relatives of the deceased came from miles around to pay respect to the memory of one of their most esteemed citizens," declared the Las Vegas *Gazette*.[246]

Because of his political prominence, news of Patrón's death spread across the territory and into its border states. In lamenting his death, the Las Vegas *Gazette* called the former legislator one of the best-known young men in New Mexico, a man who "was respected and beloved" by all who knew him. The paper said his life's work was marked by intelligence, honesty and industry. Perhaps his remarkable life was best summarized by the Las Vegas *Daily Optic* in its April 14, 1884, account of his death:

Juan B. Patrón was one of the brightest and best informed young men of native descent in New Mexico and a man of unusual promise. He had been liberally educated at [St. Michael's College] and had held several positions of honor and trust, among them the speakership of the House of Representatives. A bright future was before him, and had he lived he doubtless would have made an enviable record in public affairs in New Mexico. The shock and grief over his untimely death are universal.

Juan Patrón was thirty-one when he was killed. Had he lived out his life, politicians who succeeded him believed he would have become New Mexico's first congressman when it entered the Union in 1912.[247]

CHAPTER 20

Elusive Justice

⸺◆◇◈◇◆⸺

The day after Michael Maney was jailed in Las Vegas, deputies brought the shackled cowboy before Chief Justice Samuel B. Axtell to face a preliminary charge of murder. After entering a plea of "not guilty," Maney posted a bond of ten thousand dollars and was released from jail. Axtell set his trial for August 22.

Within days after the shooting, opposing theories abounded in the press as to Maney's motive for killing Patrón, even though the newspapers and local citizens knew very little about this obscure young Texan accused of murdering one of New Mexico's rising politicians.

Before coming to the area, Maney had worked as an ordinary hand on his father's farm after clerking for two years in his uncle's store. Born on June 23, 1857, into a prestigious family in Sequin, Texas, the accused was the oldest of five brothers and had six sisters. The family patriarch was Henry Maney, a prominent lawyer who had served several terms as a district judge before becoming editor of the Pearsall *News* in Texas. Maney's mother, Mary Malinda Erskine, was a daughter of one of Seguin's pioneer families, headed by Major Michael Erskine, a renowned Indian fighter on the Texas frontier.[248]

The first to come to Maney's defense in the Las Vegas *Daily Optic* was his ranch boss, George C. Peacock, who said he and Maney were boyhood friends. "Maney has never drank liquor to excess, nor was he drunk the night he shot Patrón," the foreman declared. "I am satisfied that he would never have shot Patrón without some provocation," adding that Maney was never quarrelsome and always enjoyed a good reputation.[249]

Patrón sympathizers, however, stoutly believed that Maney was hired by the slain man's enemies to silence him because he knew about "the evil doings by some of the men" involved in the Lincoln County War. Eugenio Romero, a former Las Vegas mayor, said the consensus among county citizens was "that Maney was ordered to get Patrón out of the way, as some people did not like him." Romero said he knew Patrón drank some. "But I have never seen him intoxicated in my life," he added.[250]

Two of the men deputized to escort Maney to jail also had different opinions as to the cause of the shooting. Like most others quoted in the press, neither had been eyewitnesses to the killing. George Giddings theorized that Patrón's enemies hired Maney to pick a fight with the popular politician and kill him in the process. Giddings, too, claimed that motive for the presumed assassination stemmed from Patrón's days in Lincoln. George V. Davidson, however, laid the blame for the shooting on a "drinking spree" that led Maney and Patrón "to get into a quarrel over a trivial matter...[and] when Patrón was about to draw his weapon, Maney fired."[251]

An anonymous citizen writing in the Las Vegas *Stock Grower* challenged claims that Patrón died from an assassin's bullet. "While the circumstances do not render Maney free of a crime, they most certainly clear him of being an assassin," he said. Citing Patrón's reputation for being dangerous when drinking as "second to none," the writer asked Patrón's family and friends "not to clamor for the blood of the killer, who only lives because he was quicker than his antagonist."[252]

Maney told a Las Vegas *Daily Optic* reporter he had no previous problems with Patrón before the shooting. "I always thought a great deal of Patrón and had never had any trouble or difficulty with him," the cowboy explained. "That night, Patrón was drinking heavily, and his manner and comments caused me to think my life was in danger."[253]

In preparing for Maney's trial in August, his team of lawyers tried unsuccessfully to serve subpoenas on three material witnesses for the defense. Knowing they would be summoned to testify, William Ruth, William Owens and Thomas Jones had secretly fled to Texas to avoid court. All were under earlier indictments for gambling and feared they would be tried on those charges if they came to court. Saving their own hides, they reasoned, was more important than testifying for Maney, whom they barely knew.

Frustrated by the delay, Judge Axtell reluctantly granted Maney's lawyers a continuance to December but remanded Maney to jail without bond. The re-jailing of Maney stirred the Las Vegas *Daily Optic* to rail, "This seems to us to favor more a persecution than a legal prosecution."[254]

Axtell reconvened his court the following winter, determined to adjudicate the case. He scheduled Maney's trial for December 5, 1884. Again, defense witnesses failed to appear even though Jones had given the court a sworn affidavit the previous May. It contained his eyewitness account of the shooting. Ruth had promised to appear. However, while coming to court, he turned his horse around when discovering he left his money purse behind at a ranch eighty miles away. He never reached the courtroom. As for Owens, he was nowhere to be found. Setting aside defense pleas for a continuance, a stubborn Axtell ordered the trial to begin. Twelve men were selected as the jury—seven "native citizens" and five "Anglos." The Las Vegas *Daily Optic* considered the panel to be the best ever assembled in the county.[255]

The trial opened that morning with Attorney General William Breeden and former U.S. Attorney Thomas B. Catron in charge of the prosecution. Witnesses included Pablo Anaya, Cresenciano Gallegos, Gregorio Baros, William Giddings, Franco Trujillo and Nicholas Griego. Maney's defense team consisted of Sydney M. Barnes and the law firm of Lee & Fort, both hired by Maney's father, himself a prominent lawyer and former district judge in Texas. During the trial, Henry Maney listened intently as he assessed each ruling by Axtell and its impact on his son's case.

A steady stream of testimony and the cross-examinations of witnesses droned into the early evening. After hearing closing arguments by the opposing attorneys, the jury received its instructions from the bench. In delivering his charge, Axtell took great pains to explain the difference between premeditated murder and justifiable homicide as defined under the law. If the jury judged the killing as premeditated, Axtell instructed, it should find the accused guilty of murder in the fourth degree. Then, point-by-point, he put forth eight examples in which excusable or justifiable homicide was acceptable. Wittingly or not, he subtly steered the jury toward Maney's claim of self-defense.

"There is no retreating from a Colt revolver or Winchester rifle," Axtell expounded. "When an assailant is within striking or shooting distance and acts in such a manner as to create a positive belief in the mind of the assaulted that he is about to shoot, the assaulted may at once fire. Criminality or innocence will not depend upon the nice question, 'Who first touched the trigger?' The question is, 'Who was the assaulting party?'"[256]

The jury received the case at 9:30 p.m. deliberating past midnight, the jury members recessed and returned to court at 10 a.m. the next morning, weary and bleary-eyed. Their long deliberation proved inconclusive. The jury foreman reported to Axtell that the jurymen had agreed to disagree, producing an evenly divided jury.

It was a surprising outcome, but the Las Vegas *Daily Optic* found some consolation in the split decision. "It was indeed gratifying to learn that there was no race division in the jury," the *Optic* boasted. "Three natives and three Anglos stood for guilty, and four natives and two Anglos stood for not guilty."[257]

Had the jury found Maney guilty of murder in the fourth degree, the young cowboy would have faced between one to seven years in prison or a fine of no less than five hundred dollars. On the frontier, a man's life was not worth much more than the value of his horse.

CHAPTER 21

Maney's Escape

⬥✦⬥

Nearly a year had passed since Juan Patrón's death, and his killer had yet to be tried successfully in the courts. When the split jury in December failed to reach a verdict, Maney's attorneys seized the opportunity to win a change of venue from Las Vegas to Santa Fe. A third trial was set for July 1885.

In the meantime, Maney remained free on bond until his bondsman took an unexpected step shortly after Judge Axtell granted the venue change. Saying only that he had "good reasons," the guarantor withdrew Maney's bond and marched the cowboy to the sheriff's office in Santa Fe with no further explanation. The surprise move set off worried speculation that the bondsman believed Maney was either a flight risk or sensed a plot was brewing to bust him out of jail during the trial.[258]

To the surprise of no one, Maney and jailed thief Richard Elliott engineered a clever escape in the early evening of May 10. After having a jailhouse dinner, the two prisoners received permission to use the outside privy. Shackled in leg-irons and unguarded, they hobbled to the toilet. Worried when the duo failed to return in a reasonable time, the sheriff deputy rushed to fetch them, only to gape into an empty and stinking outhouse. His prisoners had escaped through a hole freshly cut into the privy's roof and landed in the arms of waiting friends who broke loose their shackles.[259]

Maney made a clean getaway on a horse possibly provided by one of his brothers, who had been seen earlier in the day loafing around a livery stable in town. Governor Lionel Sheldon promptly offered a five-hundred-dollar reward for Maney's recapture. A sheriff's posse spent days scouring the countryside for the two fugitives but returned empty handed.

Assuming that Maney had galloped back to Texas to avoid capture, Governor Sheldon, on September 25, 1886, sent a requisition to the governor of Texas for Maney's arrest. The request reached Austin sixteen months after Maney's escape and nearly two and one-half years after Patrón's death. The requisition warrant was never served.[260]

In the meantime, Sheriff Francesco Chavez of San Miguel County continued to receive warrants demanding Maney's appearance before each term of district court until he returned the last warrant un-served on January 29, 1889. At that point, the court threw up its hands in exasperation and stopped issuing any more warrants for Maney's arrest.

The wanted killer had successfully out-waited the court's patience. In 1890, New Mexico Governor L. Bradford Prince withdrew all offers of outstanding rewards, including the one for Michael Erskine Maney. With the reward lifted, any remote interest in recapturing the fugitive died.[261]

Yet the whereabouts of Patrón's killer remained an enduring mystery in all of the succeeding histories written about those violent days in the New Mexico Territory. Census records, however, show that Michael Erskine Maney lived happily ever after in Doña Ana County, proving an old adage that often the safest place is in the heart of danger. By 1910, Maney had settled in Doña Ana County's largest town. Populated with more than five thousand people at the time, Las Cruces provided an ideal place for Maney to hunker down as a fugitive from justice. It was a forty-mile gallop into Mexico and even a shorter dash into Texas, should he need to outrun the reach of New Mexico lawmen.[262]

After his escape, Maney may or may not have returned to Texas. Census records do show that he spent a period of time in Oklahoma in the 1890s. There, he married a woman named Barbara, who was twenty years younger. Their first child, a son named Henry Erskine, was born in Oklahoma in 1898. After moving to Las Cruces, Maney and his wife had four more children, all daughters—Alice, Agnes, Allie and Virginia.[263] As the years passed, Maney enjoyed a long, presumably peaceful life, first as a farmer and finally as a retired carpenter.

Born into a sturdy gene pool that provided most members of his family a long life, Maney died at age eighty-four on February 11, 1942. His father Henry died a widower on November 5, 1929, at the age of ninety years, eight months and eight days. Michael's mother Mary Malinda died on February 12, 1913. Like her son Michael, she was eighty-four at her death.[264]

Post-Mortem

They say it is very healthy here.
None, scarcely, die a natural death.
They don't have an opportunity.
There is too much lead in the air [265]

Rev. Taylor F. Ealy, March 11, 1878
Lincoln, New Mexico

Juan Patrón's violent death illustrates how whiskey and guns in the hands of hard-drinking men with hair-trigger tempers had become the bane of existence on the Western frontier in the late 1800s. In a split second that night in Moore's saloon, Patrón's life, which held so much promise, ended much like a slain hero in a Greek tragedy.

With few exceptions, men on the frontier drank nearly all of the time, and nearly all men carried guns. For most men, including errant priests, drinking and gambling provided an easy escape from the drudgery and toil of frontier life. But alcohol carries dangerous powers, too. It can bloat egos, overinflate courage and incite unreasonable resort to violence. Perilous potion, indeed![266]

John Tunstall and Alexander McSween, rarely, if ever, turned to alcohol—not that abstinence promised them long lives. All others drawn into the Lincoln County War, however, consumed whiskey regularly. Some drank heavily and constantly. Jimmy Dolan imbibed deeply, and it cost him his life in the end.

Dolan's hapless life was filled with ironies. Determined to regain his pre-war prominence in Lincoln, Dolan took over the old Tunstall store in 1882. A year later, he and his longtime friend William L. Rynerson acquired Tunstall's former ranch on the Rio Feliz and from that base built the largest cattle company in the county.[267]

Dolan also dabbled in politics, serving as county treasurer for five years and later winning election in 1888 as senator in the territorial legislature. Despite his prominence, he never found happiness in life. His first wife, Caroline Fritz, died shortly after their second daughter was born. Then he hastily married his children's caretaker, Maria Whitlock. Rumors persisted that he mistreated her throughout their troubled marriage, and he turned to ninety-proof liquor to assuage his own misery.

Like his business mentor, Lawrence Murphy, Dolan eventually became a pitiful drunk. "The saloon men would not let him have whiskey, but the cowboys would give it to him," Frank Coe recalled. Dolan died in Roswell in 1898 from the ravages of alcoholism at age forty-nine.[268]

Not all fighters in the war ended up poorly. Cousins Frank and George Coe turned away from violence and settled on a spread they called Glencoe on the middle Ruidoso. As they prospered, their family grew into an expansive dynasty that flourished socially and politically well into New Mexico's early statehood.[269]

George Peppin, Yginio Salazar and John Copeland also lived long, productive lives in the peaceful years that followed. Captain Saturnino Baca, longtime friend and political mentor to Patrón, lived longer than any of them. He and his wife, Juanita, with their nine children, settled into ranch life near Lincoln. In 1889, a dispute over grazing rights disrupted their quiet life. In an exchange of gunfire, Baca took a bullet in the arm and eventually lost it to a surgeon's saw. Unbowed, this tough little pioneer, who gave birth to Lincoln County as a legislator, lived to be ninety-four. He died in 1924.[270]

Dolan's earlier business partner, John H. Riley, fared better in life than his old friend. Never known for bravery, Riley was conspicuously absent during the deadliest fighting in the Lincoln County War. After the conflict, he settled in Las Cruces, married Annie Cuniffe in 1882 and abandoned his family twelve years later for Colorado. He prospered first as a cattle grower and then owned one of Colorado's prized hog farms. Riley died February 10, 1916, of pneumonia at age sixty-five—four decades after he cowardly shot Patrón in the back, crippling him for life.[271]

Another whose addiction to whiskey muddled his judgment was Lieutenant Colonel Nathan Dudley, who erratically engaged his Fort Stanton troops in the war. Having survived an embarrassing court-martial instigated by Governor Lew Wallace, the beleaguered officer was shunted off to Fort Union in late 1879. Through sheer staying power in the army, seniority enabled him to retire as a full colonel in 1889. Dudley lived out his final years in Roxbury, Massachusetts and died in 1910 at eighty-five.[272]

After the army vacated Fort Stanton in 1890, its facilities were used for a variety of missions over the next 120 years. In 1893, it housed a Merchant Marine tuberculosis hospital, which operated until 1966 when it became a state hospital and training center for the mentally handicapped. It operated until 1995. During World War II, old troop barracks were reopened and housed German prisoners of war and the civilian crew of Nazi Germany's prized superliner, the *SS Columbus*. In 2008, the state designated the old frontier fort a New Mexico State Monument and celebrates its past in an annual festival.[273]

As Juan Patrón expanded his business in Puerto de Luna, John Chisum began dismantling his cattle empire. After the war, the "Cattle King on the Pecos" sold off most of his herds. What little cattle remained sustained him until his creditors and nagging lawsuits slowly whittled his wealth down to a financial nub. While dealing with his legal battles, Chisum faced a more serious problem. A drug-resistant neck tumor launched cancer throughout his body. Eight months after Patrón was killed, the once powerful cowman died, on December 22, 1884 at an Arkansas health resort. He was sixty.[274]

A small herd of cattle that Chisum supposedly gave to Sue McSween set the spirited widow onto the path of becoming a "cattle queen" in her own right. After settling her husband's estate in 1880, she married George Barber, a surveyor reading law under the tutelage of Ira Leonard. Together, they plunged into raising stock on a large scale in 1885 on their ranch at Three Rivers near White Oaks.[275]

While her husband practiced law in White Oaks and Lincoln, Sue busily managed the ranch with eight thousand cattle, supervising construction of buildings, fences and corrals while overseeing her cowboys and farmhands. Her fame as a successful stock grower and woman boss of Three Rivers Ranch spread beyond New Mexico and as far as New York City. She proved to be an able, strong-willed and independent woman in an era when woman were expected to be timid and obedient.

In 1891, Sue divorced Barber on grounds he abandoned her, but she continued to operate the ranch until 1902, when she sold it and moved into a house in White Oaks. As her small fortune dwindled, she aged into a bitter, whining and mean-spirited old woman. Historian Maurice G. Fulton tried to extract her valuable recollections about the war but for all his courtly patience ended up with a pile of rambling, worthless letters. Not once in them did she ever express gratitude to Juan Patrón for housing her after her own large abode lay in ashes. Nearly penniless, she died in 1931 at the age of eighty-six.

Beatriz Patrón was another woman who persevered in the wake of her husband's violent death. Widowed at twenty-six, faced with raising three small children alone and emotionally crushed by her loss, Beatriz battled depression for a while but rebounded with the help of her tightly knit family. Lorenzo Labadie and his wife, Rallitos, embraced the young Patrón family and provided Beatriz and her children permanent residence in the sprawling Labadie ranch house near Santa Rosa. From there, Beatriz successfully managed the Agua Negra orchard a few miles away, while Juan Patrón's partner, William Giddings, assumed control of their Puerto de Luna business interests.

After her children left home and started their own families, Beatriz, at age forty-nine, married Estolano Ortega, a sixty-year-old widower, on April 15, 1907, in Puerto de Luna. As she and Estolano entered Our Lady of Refuge Church to exchange marital vows that day, each gave a doleful nod towards where Juan Patrón's body lay beneath the vestibule floor. The couple's marriage ended with Estolano's death on February 11, 1927, at seventy-nine. After being twice widowed, Beatriz retook her maiden name and lived out her life in Santa Rosa. On March 3, 1945, she died at age eighty-seven.[276]

Though married a short time, the Patróns spawned an impressive family tree. Their first daughter, Rayitos, in her marriage to Juan Hinojos, had ten children, seven of whom survived. Like her father, she became a schoolteacher and eventually won election as superintendent of schools in Guadalupe County. Her younger sister, Dolores, nicknamed Lola, also taught in Santa Rosa schools and raised five children in her marriage to Alberto A. Tipton. On September 25, 1962, while walking on a residential sidewalk, Lola was struck by a car backing out of a driveway and killed. She was seventy-eight and survived by her children and six grandchildren. Three years later, Rayitos died in Albuquerque on July 31, 1965 after a short illness, leaving behind six surviving children, fifteen grandchildren and thirty-seven great-grandchildren. She was eighty-five.[277]

Juan Patrón's only son and namesake struck out for the border towns of Mexico after completing his education at St. Michael's College. Below the border, he learned pharmacy and married Guadalupe Sanchez, a native Mexican. The couple later moved to Los Angeles before settling in San

Diego. Their marriage produced a daughter, Mary Eva, and a son, Charles, who became the first of three Patrón descendants ordained as Catholic priests, reminiscent of a wish Archbishop Lamy had for the young Juan Patrón while attending St. Michael's College. The other two Patrón priests were the Reverend William Sanchez and the Reverend John Brasher. The Patrón siblings combined had six children and eight grandchildren. Juan Jr. died February 28, 1962, at eighty.[278]

During his religious tenure, Lamy advanced education dramatically throughout his pastoral domain after opening those first schools in Santa Fe. Like Patrón, many of Lamy's students became noted political figures in the territory. From its earliest years, St. Michael's College rightly boasted that nearly every public office in New Mexico had been held at one time or another by an alumnus. In 1947, the college relocated to a larger facility, enabling it to offer an accredited program of higher education. In 1966, the school was renamed the College of Santa Fe and remained under control of the De Salle Christian Brothers. In 2008, the religious order yielded operational control to a private corporation. Two years later, the college renamed itself the Santa Fe University of Art & Design.[279]

As age began to sap Archbishop Lamy's energies, the seventy-three-year-old prelate asked to be relieved of his duties. On July 18, 1885, Pope Leo XIII accepted his resignation. Lamy eased into a quiet retirement with long walks, welcoming admiring callers and tending to his beloved garden. In 1888, the old priest became sick with pneumonia. On Feb. 12, Lamy fell into a restorative sleep and died during the early hours of the next morning. Within hours, all of the bells of Santa Fe rang out, and everyone hearing their doleful message knew for whom they tolled.[280]

The life of Juan Patrón's oldest sister, Juana, remains a mystery. As Mexican tradition dictated, running the family household fell on Juana's shoulders after her mother's death sometime before 1870. Juana was about twenty when she assumed those tasks and presumably continued as woman of the house for her father and siblings until Isidro Patrón's murder in December 1873 when the Horrell brothers shot up her sister's wedding dance. After her father's death, her life faded into the mist of history. No records have been found to say whether Juana ever married, had children, or lived a long or short life. Baptized November 19, 1845, she was thirty-nine when her brother Juan was killed.

Juan Patrón's younger sister, Encarnacion, and her husband, Rafael Gutierrez, settled in Tularosa shortly after their marriage. Built like a fortress, the couple's home had a walled compound where Mescalero

Apaches from a nearby reservation came weekly to trade their meats and sheep hides with the Gutierrez's. On occasion, Billy the Kid stopped by for a meal, favoring Encarnacion's freshly made corn tortillas, which he would stuff into his pants pockets.

Encarnacion and Rafael had four children. In 1895, Rafael, a rancher and gold miner, died from a burst appendix. Six years after his death, Encarnacion married John P. Meadows, remembered as an inept sheriff deputy in Doña Ana County. During their stormy five-year marriage, Meadows spent and drank through Encarnacion's financial holdings left behind by her first husband. When they divorced, the baby sister to whom a youthful Juan Patrón had read stories was so destitute she took in laundry to pay her bills. Encarnacion died on Christmas Day in 1929 at her daughter Juanita's home in El Paso. She was seventy-three.[281]

Patrón's father-in-law, Lorenzo Labadie, remained active as patriarch of a family dynasty that remained woven into the political fabric of the territory for many years. In November 1892, the spry seventy-year-old rancher ran for election to the legislature from Guadalupe County against Celso Baca, the fifty-six-year-old founder of Santa Rosa. It turned into a bitter contest between two widely known pioneers. When the ballots were tallied, Baca had won by seventy-six votes. Labadie protested, claiming his supporters were turned away at the polls illegally and that some Baca supporters voted without being legally registered.

When the legislature convened on December 26, it seated Baca as a sworn member of the house. Labadie carried his protest to Santa Fe on January 3 and challenged Baca's right to be seated. After reviewing Labadie's complaint and Baca's defense, a house committee ruled on February 2 that Baca be unseated and that Labadie take his place as the duly-elected representative. The house upheld the committee ruling by a twelve-to-ten vote. The outcome nearly caused the two county elders to exchange blows, but they were pulled apart in time.[282]

Lorenzo Labadie died on his birthday in 1904 at eighty-one. He passed on to his son Tranquilino a lifetime spirit for public service. After serving as the legislature's official interpreter when Patrón was speaker of the house in 1879, Tranquilino progressed steadily through the government ranks of the city of Las Vegas and San Miguel and Guadalupe counties. In 1910, he served on the New Mexico Convention that wrote a new constitution for the territory, enabling it to join the Union. On January 6, 1912, New Mexico became the forty-seventh state. That year, Labadie served in New Mexico's first state legislature, representing Guadalupe County. Patrón's cherished friend died the next year on May 29, 1913, at the age of fifty-nine.[283]

A month before Patrón's death, the two best friends celebrated Labadie's marriage to Florentina Romero on March 8, 1884, in Las Vegas. That day, Patrón joined a throng of happy faces on the steps of Our Lady of Sorrows Church as they cheered the exiting newlyweds for an evening of gaiety. It was the last time *los mejores amigos* saw each other. Thirty days later, Patrón lay dead with a hole through his heart on the dirt floor of a Puerto de Luna saloon.[284]

The only family members to witness Patrón's shooting death were Roman Labadie and Cresenciano Gallegos. Each moved on with his life after the tragic loss of their brother-in-law. After taking a turn at farming, Roman went into law enforcement, working as a deputy sheriff in Guadalupe and San Miguel Counties. In 1911, he won election to Guadalupe County's first board of commissioners to work under the seal of statehood. Roman died in 1931 at seventy. Gallegos, a stock rancher and husband of Dolores Labadie, turned his interest to newspapering in 1902 when he and partner W. C. Burnett managed the *Guadalupe County Democrat*. In 1905, they sold the paper, and Gallegos won election to the territorial senate. He died in Santa Rosa in 1919 at sixty-three.[285]

If Juan Patrón and Billy Bonney ever met again after Patrón held the young outlaw in protective custody for twenty-seven days in his Lincoln store, no record has ever been found. Their paths parted for good on June 27, 1879. Smarting from Governor Lew Wallace's unfulfilled promise of a pardon, Billy the Kid walked out of Patrón's makeshift jail unchallenged and resumed a life of crime.

Months later, Wallace would write those sweet words, "The End," to his biblical epic of *Ben Hur: A Tale of the Christ*. Its publication in late 1880 made Wallace a rich and admired literary figure. It also won him a presidential appointment as U.S. minister to the court of the Turkish sultan in Constantinople in May 1881.

In the meantime, Billy and his boys embarked on a two-year rampage of robbing settlers and rustling stock across New Mexico. Their crime spree finally came to an end in December 1880 at Stinking Springs when Sheriff Deputy Pat Garrett captured the gang. At his trial, Billy was found guilty in the murder of Sheriff William Brady, handed a death sentence and hauled in chains from Mesilla to Lincoln to await hanging.

When Garrett, the newly elected sheriff, took custody of the Kid on April 21, 1881, he confined him in a second-floor room in the county courthouse that once stood as the Murphy-Dolan house of tyranny. Garrett assigned deputies Bob Olinger and J.W. Bell to guard the notorious outlaw, which spelled trouble for the Kid. He detested Olinger, a tall, powerful bully who enjoyed tormenting his prisoner.

On April 28, while Olinger escorted other prisoners across the street to the Wortley Hotel for their noon meal, Billy overpowered Bell, grabbed a pistol and fired twice at the deputy on the staircase. The first shot missed. The second round ricocheted off a wall and tore through Bell's torso below the left arm. The Kid then picked up Olinger's shotgun and ran to an upstairs window facing the street. Surprised by the gun shots across the street, Olinger sprinted toward the courthouse, only to see his own double-barreled shotgun aimed at him from the second floor window. Before he could react, the gun exploded and Olinger, known as the "tall Sycamore," was cut down and died with a chest full of buckshot.

Three months after Billy's escape, Pat Garrett and his deputies tracked the outlaw down in Fort Sumner. On the night of July 14, 1881, Garrett crept silently into the bedroom of Pete Maxwell and in a whisper asked him the whereabouts of his friend Billy. Before the awakened man could answer the intruder, Billy entered the darkened room and asked in Spanish, *"Quien es? Quien es?"* Sensing it was the Kid, Garrett fired twice. The first bullet pierced Billy's chest just above the heart, and the twenty-one-year-old desperado slumped to the floor and died. The sheriff's second shot had gone wild.[286]

Newspapers across the land trumpeted Billy Bonney's death. In headlines, the young outlaw had joined the pantheon of America's most feared desperados as a cold-blooded murderer, notorious for killing more men than anyone his age. Almost at once, he was enshrined in the folklore of America. Over time, a steady flow of books and movies, mostly all devoid of historical accuracy, followed. They forever cemented the legend of Billy the Kid in America's imagination. Every August, a reenactment of his daring escape attracts thousands of visitors to the small, sleepy village of Lincoln, now one of New Mexico's popular state monuments.

In another small village, miles away from Lincoln, another more modest monument stands in Puerto de Luna. It is the small brownstone church of Our Lady of Refuge, which sits atop the burial ground of Juan Patrón. As worshipers enter the church, they may choose to remember the life of a young boy who rose out of peasantry like a phoenix to lead New Mexico's first generation of governments during its most violent period. Sadly, his ascending star crashed before it reached the heights promised by his accomplishments.

Our Lady of Refuge Church in Puerto de Luna in 2009

THE END

ENDNOTES

Abbreviations

DIL	Department of Interior Library, Washington D.C.
HHC	Haley Memorial Library and History Center, Midland, Texas
HL	Huntington Library, San Marino, California
IHS	Indiana Historical Society
LCHS	Lincoln County Historical Society
NARA	National Archives and Records Administration, Washington D.C.
NMSRCA	New Mexico State Records Center and Archives, Santa Fe
UAL	University of Arizona Library, Tucson

Chapter 1

[1] Paul Horgan, *Lamy of Santa Fe*, (New York, Farrar, Straus and Giroux, 1975), 29. Horgan's work is the definitive biography of Archbishop Lamy, dating from his childhood in France to his death in Santa Fe.

[2] Ibid, 73.

[3] Ibid, 77-80.

[4] Ibid, 12.

[5] Ibid, 107.

[6] Ibid, 128.

[7] Ibid, 128. Also see Calvin A. and Susan A. Roberts, *New Mexico* (Albuquerque, University of New Mexico Press, 2006), 186.

[8] Horgan, 127, 186.

[9] Norman J. Bender, *Missionaries, Outlaws and Indians: Taylor F. Ealy at Lincoln and Zuni, 1878-1881*, (Albuquerque, University of New Mexico Press), 23.

[10] Baptism record of Juan Bautista Patrón at age five days on November 25, 1852, at St. Francis Cathedral, Santa Fe. Discovered by author at NMSRCA on microfilm

roll 152 (LDS-Mormon). Heretofore, Patrón's birth had been estimated at between 1850 and 1853. Some historians confused his birth date with that of an earlier son born to Patrón's parents. That son was christened Juan Bautista Patrón on January 11, 1850, but died in infancy.

[11] Horgan, 181.

[12] Ibid, 377.

[13] Santa Fe *Daily New Mexican*, November 18, 1865.

Chapter 2

[14] Horgan, 181.

[15] St. Michael's College's first hundred years is recounted in a 1959 *Centennial Year Book* on file in the archives of its successor, Santa Fe University of Art & Design.

[16] Horgan, 272, 283.

[17] Santa Fe *Daily New Mexican*, February 13, 1864.

[18] Horgan, See photo after 140.

[19] St. Michael's College, 1959 *Centennial Year Book*.

[20] *Daily New Mexican*, Santa Fe, June 14, 1912.

Chapter 3

[21] U.S. censuses for 1850, 1860 and 1870 listed Isidro Patrón as a farm owner first in Santa Fe and later in Lincoln.

[22] Robert M. Utley, *High Noon in Lincoln: Violence on the Western Frontier* (Albuquerque, University of New Mexico Press, 1987), 11.

[23] Lincoln had no schools, churches, hotels or restaurants. Visitors either camped in their wagons or stayed with friends. Freight was hauled in by ox-team or mule team, making all goods not grown locally expensive.

[24] Horgan, See 121 for description of a typical adobe home in the 1870s. The Patrón home has been restored over the years, is listed on the National Register of Historic Places and is owned by Cleis and Jeremy Jordan. Until recently, it was a bed & breakfast destination known as Casa de Patrón.

[25] Billy Charles Patrick Cummings, *Frontier Parish: Recovered Catholic History of Lincoln County, 1860-1884* (Lincoln, Lincoln County Historical Publications, 1995). Cummings painstakingly combed through scattered parish records to reconstruct the Catholic Church's earliest years in Lincoln County.

[26] Miguel Antonio Otero, *My Life on the Frontier, 1882-1897*, a facsimile of original 1939 edition (Santa Fe, Sunstone Press, 2007), 47-52. Otero provides vivid accounts of the Penitentes' bloody rituals.

[27] Cummings, 10-11.

[28] See miscellaneous material in Patrón biographical notes, Mullen Collection, HHC. They state that Patrón was Lincoln's first schoolteacher.

Chapter 4

[29] Frederick W. Nolan, *The Lincoln County War, A Documentary History* (Norman, University of Oklahoma Press, 1992), provides the most definitive account of the rise of the House of Murphy beginning on page 32.

[30] Utley, 14, for a brief account of Murphy's business practices. The citizen quoted is Florencio Gonzalez from his deposition in Frank Warner Angel, "Report on the Death of John H. Tunstall," Department of Justice, 1878. The Angel Report, herein cited as such, is in the NARA.

[31] Lily Casey Klasner, *My Girlhood Among Outlaws*, Ed. Eve Ball (Tucson, University of Arizona Press, 1972), 98.

[32] Maurice Garland Fulton, *History of the Lincoln County War*, Ed. Robert N. Mullin (Tucson, University of Arizona Press 1968), 29-31. I have relied on Fulton's account of the incendiary killing of two Hispanic ranch hands by John H. Copeland and John H. Riley because of its detail and Patrón's role in trying to bring the killers to justice. See Chapter 3 "Continued Lawlessness—1875."

[33] Frederick W. Nolan, *Bad Blood: The Life and Times of the Horrell Brothers* (Stillwater, Oklahoma, Barbed Wire Press, 1995) p. 57. Juan Gonzales also gained notoriety for recruiting the first American prostitute to Lincoln. See 168 for a brief biography.

[34] *Daily New Mexican*, Santa Fe, February 9, 1873.

[35] Nolan, *Lincoln County War*, 49.

[36] Nolan, *Bad Blood*, 44-45. Lincoln County election results, November 1875, NMSRCA.

Chapter 5

[37] Nolan, *Bad Blood*, 35.

[38] Nolan, *Lincoln County War*, 48.

[39] Ibid, 50.

[40] Ibid, 51.

[41] Ibid, 50.

[42] Nolan, *Bad Blood*, 53, *Lincoln County War*, 50-51

[43] Nolan, *Bad Blood,* 55, *Lincoln County War*, 51.

[44] Cummings, 22.

[45] Nolan, *Lincoln County War*, 51.

[46] Ibid.

[47] Patrón deposition, June 6, 1878, Angel Report, NARA.

[48] Research by Charles Munro, a great-great-grandson of Encarnacion Patrón, concluded that the wedding dance was in celebration of Encarnacion's marriage to Rafael Gutierrez. The author found no evidence to the contrary. (See Archdiocese of Santa Fe, Santa Rita Parish, Carrizozo: Marriages 1869-1956, NMSRCA.)

[49] Mark Lee Gardner, *To Hell on a Fast Horse* (New York, HarperCollins Publishers, 2010), 84, describes a typical wedding *baile* in New Mexico during this period. Gardner suggests that had Billy the Kid attended the Patrón dance, he would have asked the fiddlers to play the *gallina*, which means "chicken" in Spanish. Because native New Mexicans used the word for "wild turkey," Billy actually would have been asking to hear "Turkey in the Straw," one of his favorite dance tunes.

[50] Nolan, *Lincoln County War*, 52.

[51] Robert A. Casey, interview with J. Evetts Haley, June 25, 1937, R. N. Mullen Collection, HHC.

[52] Cummings, 22.

[53] Nolan, *Bad Blood*, 71.

[54] Ibid, 60.

[55] Ibid, 66.

[56] Ibid, 71-72.

[57] Patrón deposition, June 6, 1878, Angel Report, NARA.

[58] Klasner, 105.

[59] Nolan, *Bad Blood*, 86-87.

[60] Klasner, 105-106.

[61] Nolan, *Bad Blood*, 89.

[62] Ibid, 90.

[63] Patrón deposition, Angel Report, NARA.

Chapter 6

[64] Joel Jacobsen, *Such Men as Billy the Kid* (Lincoln, University of Nebraska, 1994), 11. Quote is attributed to Susan McSween Barber in letter to Maurice Fulton, June 27, 1926, UAL.

[65] Nolan, *Lincoln County War*, 61. Also see Lincoln County District Court records, Criminal Case #149, Territory of New Mexico vs Juan B. Patrón, April 23, 1875, NMSRCA.

66 Mesilla *News*, September 22, 1875, reported: "On Wednesday last, John H. Riley shot Juan B. Patrón at Lincoln. The buckboard driver gives the following particulars. Patrón was drunk and kept following up Riley and insulting him. Riley told Patrón to let him alone, but he refused and finally pulled out his pistol whereupon Riley took a rifle and shot Patrón, the ball entering near the spine and passing into the abdomen from which it was cut out by the physician, who says Patrón cannot live." (Philip J. Rasch Files, #54, LCHS).

67 Nolan, *Lincoln County War*, 482.

68 Patrón deposition, Angel Report, NARA.

69 Nolan, *Lincoln County War*, 73.

70 Horgan, 382.

71 Klasner, 134.

72 Ibid,135.

73 Ibid,135-136.

74 Horgan, 382.

Chapter 7

75 Utley, 7.

76 Ibid, 3.

7 Frederick W. Nolan, *The Life and Death of John Henry Tunstall* (Albuquerque, University of New Mexico Press, 1965), 190-193.

78 *Lincoln County Board of Commissioners Journal*, February 12, 1877, Office of Lincoln County Clerk, Carrizozo, NM.

79 Before coming to New Mexico, Tunstall worked four years in Victoria British Columbia and spent several months in California in search of business opportunities.

Chapter 8

80 Nolan, *Life and Death of John Tunstall*, 192-193.

81 Nolan, *Lincoln County War*, 101.

82 Ibid, 102.

83 Utley, 27.

84 Klasner, 98.

85 Patrón deposition, Angel Report, NARA. Also see Utley, 32.

Chapter 9

[86] Nolan, *Lincoln County War*, 170. There had been local controversy over the building of the new jail. George Peppin submitted a bill for three thousand dollars to the county for building the jail. The bill later was reduced to seventeen hundred dollars and was paid. To help pay for the jail, the Patrón commission doubled license fees for merchants and saloons and raised real estate taxes by twenty-five percent (*Board of Commissioners Journal*, February 12, 1877 to July 8, 1878).

[87] Gardner, 5. The underground jail was ten feet deep and contained two cells. Its ceiling was made of logs chinked together with mud and covered with dirt. The only entrance to the jail was through a door in the floor of the jailer's two-room house above the pit.

[88] Nolan, *Lincoln County War*, 172.

[89] Ibid. Joining the breakout was Lucas Gallegos, who had been jailed for the murder of Sostero Garcia.

[90] Klasner, notes on "The Kid" for her memoir, reprinted in Nolan, *Lincoln County War*, 161.

[91] Klasner, 169-170.

[92] Silver City *Herald*, September 29, 1877.

[93] Silver City *Herald*, December 1, 1877.

[94] *Acts of the Legislative Assembly, Territory of New Mexico, Twenty-Third Session*, 11, 13.

[95] Daily temperatures and moistures, Santa Fe, January, 1878, recorded by National Weather Bureau.

[96] *Journal of the House of Representatives, Twenty-Third Legislative Session, Territory of New Mexico*, herein subsequently referred to as the House Journal.

Chapter 10

[97] House Journal.

[98] Ibid.

[99] *General Incorporation Act, Railroads* (Chapter I, Titles 2-5), herein referred to as the Railroad Act.

[100] Ibid.

[101] Railroad Act, Chapter I, Title 8.

[102] Railroad Act, Chapter II.

[103] Horgan, 385.

[104] Ibid, 384-385.

[105] Ibid, 385.

[106] Donald R. Lavash, *A Journey Through New Mexico History* (Albuquerque, University of New Mexico Press, 2006), 183-184.

[107] John B. Mondragon and Ernest S. Stapleton, *Public Education in New Mexico* (Santa Fe, Sunstone Press, 2005), 17.

Chapter 11

[108] Gerald McKevitt, *Brokers of Culture: Italian Jesuits in the American West, 1884-1919* (Palo Alto, Stanford University Press, 2006), 201. John T. McGreevy, *Catholicism and American Freedom* (New York, W. W. Norton & Company, 2003), 117.

[109] House Journal,164-169, *Journal of the Legislative Council*, 42-46, both in NMSRCA. I have relied on these segments of the two journals for the political battle between the House and Governor Axtell over the issue of Jesuit education in New Mexico.

[110] Horgan, 337-338.

[111] Billy Charles Cummings, *Patrón, Axtell Fight Over Jesuits*, article published in *Los Amigos,* July 1995, Lincoln County Heritage Trust newsletter.

[112] Sister M. Lillian Owens, S. L., Ph.D., *Jesuit Beginnings in New Mexico, 1867-1882* (El Paso, Revista Catolica Press, 1950), 66-70.

[113] Cummings, *Los Amigos* article.

[114] *New York Times*, February 26, 1879.

[115] Ibid.

[116] Ibid.

[117] W. G. Ritch papers, HL.

[118] *New York Times*, February 26, 1879.

[119] House Journal.

Chapter 12

[120] Klasner,174.

[121] Gardner, 54-55.

[122] Many histories have been written about the murder of John H. Tunstall, whose death triggered the Lincon County War. Of them, I have relied mostly on Nolan's excellent documentary history of the war and Utley's highly respected *High Noon in Lincoln* because of their extraordinary primary sources.

[123] Utley, 47.

[124] Ibid (n.17), 198.

125 Rynerson letter, Las Cruces, February 14, 1878, Lew Wallace Papers, IHS.

126 Frank Coe, interview with J. Evetts Haley, San Patricio, NM, August 14, 1927, HHC.

127 Utley, 52.

128 Ibid.

129 McSween letter to J. P. Tunstall, February 23, 1878, shown in Nolan, *Lincoln County War*, pp. 204-208.

130 Gardner, 66.

131 Ibid, 67.

132 George Coe, *Frontier Fighter: The Autobiography of George W. Coe Who Fought and Rode with Billy the Kid*, Ed. D. B. Nunis, Jr. (Chicago, The Lakeside Press, 1984), 132.

133 *Lincoln County Commission Journal, 1877-1878*, p.16, County Clerk Office, Carrizozo, NM.

134 Utley, 60. Also see (n. 22), 203.

135 Many have written that the Kid was wounded while stooping over Brady. However, Gardner in *To Hell on a Fast Horse* reveals that the Reverend Dr. Thomas F. Ealy, who ran a silk handkerchief through French's wound, wrote later that Billy "was not hit." See Gardner notes, 274.

136 My narrative of the Blazer's Mill shootout relies on Gardner's account. Frank Coe in an interview with J. Evetts Haley, March 20, 1927, said Charlie Bowdre delivered the fatal shot to Roberts. However, Gardner believes the fatal shot came from the Kid, based on written accounts by the Blazer family. See Gardner notes, 274.

137 Frank Coe, interview with J. Evetts Haley, San Patricio, NM, March 20, 1927, HHC.

138 County Commission Journal, April 10, 1878.

139 Jacobsen, 149.

140 Ibid.

141 Ibid, 150-152.

Chapter 13

142 *Mesilla Valley Independent*, April 13, 1878.

143 Jacobsen, 153.

144 Ibid.

145 Ibid, 154.

146 Ibid, 153-154.

[147] Maurice G. Fulton, *History of the Lincoln County War*, Ed. Robert N. Mullin (Tucson, University of Arizona Press, 1968),. 207.

[148] *Mesilla Valley Independent*, May 4, 1878.

[149] County Commission Journal, June 1, 1878.

[150] Ibid, 30-31.

[151] The Patrón letter, June 10, 1878, the Dudley letter, June 11, 1878, and affidavit, June 11, 1878, are from the Rasch Files, LCHS. Also see Nolan, *The Lincoln County War*, 304.

[152] Patrón letters to Dudley, both dated June 24, 1878, Rasch Files, LCHS.

[153] County Commission Journal, June 26 and July 8, 1878.

Chapter 14

[154] Nolan, *Lincoln County War*, 315 and Utley, 93. My narrative of the big battle is drawn mostly from the accounts provided by Nolan and Utley, based on their primary sources.

[155] Utley, 100.

[156] Fearing for his life, Patrón had fled to Fort Stanton and was granted safe refuge by Colonel Dudley.

[157] Folliard's surname has been published incorrectly as O'Folliard for over a century with two exceptions, first by Pat Garrett who correctly identified the boy as Tom O. Folliard and the other being Gardner in *To Hell on a Fast Horse*. Even Patrón identified him as O'Folliard in his affidavit to receive payment for holding William Bonney, Folliard and Doc Scurlock under house arrest.

[158] Utley, 104.

[159] Nolan, *Lincoln County War*, 330, 333. Also see (note 8), 565.

Chapter 15

[160] Utley, 112.

[161] Nolan, *Lincoln County War*, 348.

[162] Ibid, 319.

[163] Utley, 117.

[164] Copies printed in English and Spanish are in the Wallace Papers, IHS.

[165] County Commission Journal, October 13, 1878.

[166] Fulton, 295.

[167] Copy of Davis letter, Rasch Files, LCHS.

[168] Utley,130.

[169] Coe, 200.

[170] *Mesilla Valley Independent*, July 5, 1879.

[171] Nolan, *Lincoln County War*, 375.

[172] All of the dialogue is drawn from Fulton, 326.

[173] *Mesilla Valley Independent*, July 5, 1879.

[174] Kimball's request to Dudley, February 19, 1879, Dudley Court Records, NARA. Signers of the petition represent those citizens remaining in Lincoln at the time. Besides Patrón and Kimball, others signatories were J. B. Wilson, Ben Ellis, Jose Montano, Doctor Gurney, Susan McSween, Sam Corbet, Sidney Wilson, J. A. Tomlinson, A. J. Ballard, Saturnino and Bonifacio Baca, Lee Kayser, Esteban Chavez, David Easton, John Copeland, Santiago Mes y Trujillo, Anton Jose Garcia, W. H. Wilson, Edgar Walz, G. S. Redman and Francisco Romero y Valencia.

[175] Utley, 134-135, raises the specter of Chapman possibly being targeted for assassination by Campbell, based on a report by the *Mesilla Valley Independent*, July 5, 1879, which declared that the peace conference between the Kid and Dolan "was a sham, gotten up to throw people off guard in order, as Campbell said, to 'make a killing.'"

Chapter 16

[176] Utley,139.

[177] Ibid, 141.

[178] *Mesilla Valley Independent*, April 12, 1879.

[179] Wallace to Schurz, March 31, 1879, Wallace Papers, IHS.

[180] Wallace to Hatch, March 6, 1879, Wallace Papers, IHS.

[181] Bonney's letter to Wallace set off a famous exchange of letters between the two men. His letter, now on display at the Museum of New Mexico, is printed in full in Nolan, *Lincoln County War*, 382. The others referred to in this chapter are in the Wallace Papers, IHS.

[182] Nolan, *Lincoln County War*, 383.

[183] Wallace to Patrón, March 15, 1879, Records of the Territorial Governors, NMSRCA.

[184] The militia's official roster is in the Territorial Archives, NMSRCA and printed in Fulton, 340.

[185] Nolan, *Lincoln County War*, 383.

[186] Wallace to Patrón, March 19, 1879, Wallace Papers, IHS.

[187] Gardner, 85.

[188] Miguel Antonio Otero, Jr., *The Real Billy the Kid* (Houston, Arte Publico Press, 1998), 64.

189 Wallace notes from Bonney interview, March 23, 1879, Wallace Papers, IHS.

190 William A. Keleher, *Violence in Lincoln County, 1869-1881*(Albuquerque, University of New Mexico Press, 1957), 215-216.

191 Otero, *The Real Billy the Kid*, 64.

192 Keleher, 215.

193 Ibid, 216.

194 Wallace to Schurz, April 1, 1879, Wallace Papers, IHS.

195 Patrón to Ellis, April 12, 1879, Wallace Papers, IHS.

196 Nolan, *Lincoln County War*, 387.

197 Patrón affidavit, November 12, 1880, Lincoln County Clerk's Office, Carrizozo. Prisoners listed: William Bonney, Tom O'Folliard, Doc Scurlock and Lucas Gallegos.

198 Wallace report to Legislative Assembly in 1879, requesting appropriations to pay members of the Lincoln County Riflemen. The militia's campaign records are in the Territorial Archives, NMSRCA.

199 Wallace to Schurz, June 11, 1879, Wallace Papers, IHS.

200 See provisions of *Chapter 39, Laws of 1880, New Mexico Statutes.*

201 Ellis and Montano invoices, militia campaign records, Territorial Archives, NMSRCA.

Chapter 17

202 Cummings, *Frontier Parish,* pp. 39-40.

203 Ibid.

204 Marc Simmons, Trail Dust column, *Santa Fe Reporter*, November 30, 1988.

205 Rayitos Patrón Hinojos, written recollections, undated, NMSRCA.

206 J. J. Clancy to Maurice G. Fulton, Anton Chico, NM, November 26, 1932, Mullin Collection, HHC.

207 Daniel Flores, *Puerto de Luna* (privately published, 2010), 46.

208 *Report of the Commissioner of Indian Affairs, 1876*, p. 108, U.S. Interior Department Library, D. C.

209 Flores, 54-55.

210 Ibid, 107.

211 James East to Judge William H. Burgess, Douglas, AZ, May 20, 1926, Mullin Collection, HHC. (Also see Gardner's notes, 281.)

212 U.S.census, 1880, Fort Sumner District, NM.

Chapter 18

213 Simons, Trail Dust column, *Santa Fe Reporter*, February 1, 1989.

214 The marriages and children of Lorenzo Labadie and Domingo Labadie are listed in the records of the Hispanic Genealogical Research Center, Albuquerque, NM.

215 "La Tules," by April Kopp, *New Mexico Magazine,* October, 1991.

216 Ibid.

217 Santa Fe *New Mexican*, August 30, 1959.

218 Simons, Trail Dust column, *Santa Fe Reporter*, February 1, 1989.

219 Ibid.

220 Labadie to J. L. Collins, Superintendent of Indian Affairs, New Mexico, September 25, 1862, DIL.

221 C. L. Sonnichsen, *The Mescalero Apaches* (Norman, University of Oklahoma Press, 1979), 98-99.

222 Ibid, 101.

223 Labadie to Dr. Michael Steck, Superintendent of Indian Affairs, New Mexico, October 22, 1864, DIL.

224 Carleton to Brigadier General Lorenzo Thomas, December 23, 1863, *Condition of the Indian Tribes,* Report of Congressional Joint Special Committee, 1867, DIL

225 Steck to William P. Dole, U.S. Commissioner of Indian Affairs, December 10, 1863, DIL.

226 Carlton to Thomas, March 19, 1865, *Condition of the Indian Tribes*, 168-169, DIL

227 Carlton to Thomas, March 22, 1865, *Condition of the Indian Tribes,* 223, DIL

228 *Report of the Commissioner of Indian Affairs for 1869*, 244-245, DIL

229 *Report of the Commissioner of Indian Affairs for 1876*, 108-109, DIL

Chapter 19

230 First District Court criminal docket, case no. 1657 (Sunday liquor sales), case 1665 (carrying a pistol) and case no. 1667 (assault in a menacing manner). The three cases were adjudicated before Judge Axtell on March 20, 1884. Because the latter two case files are missing in NMSRCA, no details could be found as to whom Patrón allegedly assaulted in a menacing manner and for what reason. After Patrón won his acquittal, Axtell order that he be reimbursed for the cost of presenting his defense. Considered a "brilliant jurist" by some, Axtell also had his detractors. Many found his methods dictatorial. He often threw out jury verdicts

when he did not agree with them, supposedly in the interest of securing justice. Source: Wikipedia.

[231] Rayitos Patrón Hinojos to L. A. Ketring, Jr., August 2, 1962, Mullin Collection, HHC.

[232] The narrative from this point forward to the fatal shooting of Patrón is based on Maney's extensive interview in the Las Vegas *Daily Optic*, April 13, 1884, and affidavits sworn before Judge Axtell by Thomas Jones and William Ruth, May 2, 1884. The affidavits are in the files of the First District Court criminal case 2056 (Territory of New Mexico vs. Michael E. Maney, charge of murder), NMSRCA.

[233] The dialogue between Patrón and Maney is taken from the sworn affidavit by Thomas Jones, who said he was sitting at an open window and heard the verbal exchange between the two men just "five steps off the south end of the saloon." See First District Court case 2056 files, NMSRCA.

[234] Las Vegas *Daily Optic*, April 13, 1884. Maney cites Owens's warning about Patrón in his newspaper interview.

[235] Gregorio Baros testimony at inquest held by Justice of the Peace Pablo Anaya, 2 a.m., April 8, 1884, NMSRCA.

[236] Thomas affidavit, criminal case 2056 files, NMSRCA.

[237] Ruth affidavit, criminal case 2056 files, NMSRCA.

[238] Ibid.

[239] Las Vegas *Daily Optic*, April 13, 1884.

[240] Hinojos to Ketring, August 2, 1962.

[241] Maney testimony at inquest before Justice Anaya, NMSRCA.

[242] Las Vegas *Daily Optic*, April 13, 1884.

[243] Clancy to Fulton, November 26, 1932, Mullin Collection, HHC.

[244] Las Vegas *Daily Optic*, April 9, 1884.

[245] Our Lady of Refuge bulletin, undated, in author's file.

[246] Las Vegas *Gazette*, April 13, 1884.

[247] Miguel Antonio Otero, *My Life on the Frontier, 1882-1897* (Santa Fe, Sunstone Press, 2007, facsimile of original 1939 edition), 141-142.

Chapter 20

[248] Andrew Jackson Sowell, *Early Settlers and Indian Fighters of Southwest Texas* (Austin, State House Press, 1986), 683-691.

[249] Reprint of Las Vegas *Daily Optic* article, *New Mexican Review*, April 14, 1884.

[250] Las Vegas *Daily Optic*, April 12, 1884.

[251] *New Mexican Review*, April 14, 1884

[252] White Oaks *Golden Era*, April 24, 1884 (reprint of letter in Las Vegas *Stock Grower*).

[253] Las Vegas *Daily Optic*, April 12, 1884.

[254] Las Vegas *Daily Optic*, August 23, 1884.

[255] Las Vegas *Daily Optic*, December 4, 1884. The jurors were identified as Ramon Samora, Manuel Seguar, Juan Aragon, Gregario Aragon, Juan Baca, Pablo Mais, Doroteo Sandoval, William Frank, W. A. Givens, F. Adams, Sr., N.L. Rosenthal and H. S. Wooster.

[256] Axtell's instructions, December 5, 1884, criminal case 2056, NMSRCA.

[257] Las Vegas *Daily Optic*, December 6, 1884.

Chapter 21

[258] *New Mexican Review,* March 17, 1885.

[259] Rasch, "The Murder of Juan Patrón" (*Corral Dust*, July 1960), Mullin Collection, HHC.

[260] Elma A. Medearis letter to Rasch, October 9, 1959, Rasch Files, LCHS.

[261] Ibid.

[262] U.S. censuses 1910, 1920, 1930, Doña Ana County, NM, NARA.

[263] Ibid.

[264] Ancestry.com, Texas Death Index, 1903-2000 (database online), New Mexico Death Index, 1889-1945.

[265] Postmortem Ealy diary, March 11, 1878, Ealy Papers, special collection, UAL.

[266] Keleher, 15. Utley, 176.

[267] Dolan biographical notes, Mullin Collection, HHC.

[268] Frank Coe interview with J. Evetts Haley, San Patricio, NM, March 20, 1927, HHC.

[269] Wilbur Coe, *Ranch on the Ruidoso: The Story of a Pioneer Family in New Mexico, 1871-1968* (New York, Alfred A. Knopf, 1968).

[270] Baca biographical notes, Mullin Collection, HHC.

[271] Fulton, chapter 53.

[272] Utley,169.

[273] Fort Stanton Research notes by Lynda A. Sanchez, LCHS. James J. McBride, *Internment of the SS Columbus Crew at Fort Stanton, 1941-1945* (Publisher: Paper Tiger, 2003), Introduction.

[274] Utley,166.

[275] Fulton,420-421.

[276] Wedding registry, Our Lady of Refuge, Puerto de Luna, NM. Deaths of Beatriz and Estolano Ortega, burial registry, Our Lady of Refuge. Beatriz is buried in San Jose cemetery, Santa Rosa. Estolano is buried in Santa Rosa cemetery by El Rito Creek.

277 Information drawn from family papers, U. S.census records, Our Lady of Refuge marriage and burial registries. Rayitos Hinojos death, Santa Rosa *News,* August 5, 1965. Dolores Tipton death, Albuquerque *Tribune,* September 16, 1962.

278 Author's collection.

279 Calvin and Susan Roberts, *New Mexico* (Albuquerque, University of New Mexico Press, 2006),113. 1959 *Centennial Year Book,* St. Michael's College. Institutional history, Wikipedia.

280 Horgan, *Lamy of Santa Fe,* p. 438.

281 Encarnacion's short biography by her great-great-grandson, Chuck Munro, Prarieville, LA.

282Legislative Assembly, 30th Session, Journal of the House, 203-208, NMSRCA.

283Biographical sketch and *Proceedings of the Constitutional Convention, October 3 to November 21, 1910,* NMSRCA.

284 New Mexico marriages, 1751-1918, NMSRCA.

285 Roman Labadie biographical sketch, NMSRCA. Gallegos biographical sketch, Genealogy Trails.

286 Gardner,169-172.

BIBLIOGRAPHY

Anaya, A. P. "Paco." *I Buried Billy*. Edited by James H. Earle. College Station, TX: Creative Publishing Company, 1991.

Bender, Norman J. *Missionaries, Outlaws and Indians: Taylor F. Ealy at Lincoln and Zuni, 1878-1881*. Albuquerque: University of New Mexico Press, 1984.

Coe, George W. *Frontier Fighter: The Autobiography of George W. Coe Who Fought and Rode with Billy the Kid*. Edited by D. B. Nunis Jr. Chicago: The Lakeside Press, 1984.

Coe, Wilbur. *Ranch on the Ruidoso: The Story of a Pioneer Family in New Mexico, 1871-1968*. New York: Alfred A. Knopf, 1968.

Cummings, Billy Charles Patrick. *Frontier Parish: Recovered Catholic History of Lincoln County, 1860-1884*. Lincoln: Lincoln County Historical Publications, 1995.

Flores, Daniel. *Puerto de Luna*. Santa Rosa, NM: Self-Published, 2010.

Fulton, Maurice G. *Maurice G. Fulton's History of the Lincoln County War*. Edited by Robert N. Mullin. Tucson: University of Arizona Press, 1968.

Gardner, Mark Lee. *To Hell on a Fast Horse*. New York: HarperCollins Publishers, 2010.

Horgan, Paul. *Lamy of Santa Fe*. New York: Farrar, Straus and Giroux, 1975.

Jacobsen, Joel. *Such Men as Billy the Kid*. Lincoln: University of Nebraska Press, 1994.

Keleher, William A. *The Fabulous Frontier: Twelve New Mexico Items*. Santa Fe: Rydal Press, 1945.

Keleher, William A. *Violence in Lincoln County, 1869-1881*. Albuquerque: University of New Mexico Press, 1957.

Klasner, Lily Casey, *My Girlhood Among Outlaws*. Edited by Eve Ball. Tucson: University of Arizona Press, 1972.

Lavash, Donald R. *A Journey Through New Mexico History*. Albuquerque: University of New Mexico Press, 2006.

McBride, James J. *Internment of the SS Columbus Crew at Fort Stanton, 1941-1945*. Paper Tiger Books, 2003.

McGreevy, John T. *Catholicism and American Freedom*. New York: W. W. Norton & Company, 2003.

McKevitt, Gerald. *Brokers of Culture: Italian Jesuits in the American West, 1848-1919*. Palo Alto: Stanford University Press, 2006.

Mondragon, John B. and Ernest S. Stapleton. *Public Education in New Mexico*. Santa Fe: Sunstone Press, 2005.

Nolan, Frederick W. *Bad Blood: The Life and Times of the Horrell Brothers*. Stillwater, Oklahoma: Barbed Wire Press, 1995.

Nolan, Frederick W. *The Life and Death of John Henry Tunstall*. Albuquerque: University of New Mexico Press, 1965.

Nolan, Frederick W. *The Lincoln County War: A Documentary History*. Norman: University of Oklahoma, 1992.

Otero, Miguel Antonio. *My Life on the Frontier, 1882-1897*. Reprint of 1939 edition. Santa Fe: Sunstone Press, 2007.

Otero, Miguel Antonio. *The Real Billy the Kid, With New Light on the Lincoln County War.* New York: Rufus Rockwell Wilson, Inc., 1936.

Rasch, Philip J. *Corral Dust,* July 1960. "The Murder of Juan Patrón."

Roberts, Calvin A. and Susan A. *New Mexico.* Albuquerque: University of New Mexico Press, 2006.

Sonnichsen, C. L. *The Mescalero Apaches.* Norman: University of Oklahoma Press, 1979.

Sowell, Andrew Jackson. *Early Settlers and Indian Fighters of Southwest Texas.* Austin: State House Press, 1986.

Utley, Robert M. *High Noon in Lincoln: Violence on the Western Frontier.* Albuquerque: University of New Mexico Press, 1987.

LIST OF ILLUSTRATIONS

MAPS

INDEX

S

Salazar, Yginio, 98–99, 159
San Vicente Hospital, 72
Sanches, Jose M., 70
Sanchez, Estelano, 115
Sanchez, Martin, 115
Sanchez, William (Reverend), 162
Santa Fe, New Mexico
  history of, 4
  becomes diocese, 5–6
  legislation headquarters, 58–59
  first train to branch line, 62
Sante Fe University of Art & Design, 162
Schurz, Carl (Interior Secretary), 113, 117, 118, 123
Scurlock, Doc, 100, 105, 106, 112, 118
secular vs. religious education, 71
Segovia, Manuel "The Indian", 86
Selman, John, 101
Selman Scouts, 101, 103–105
Sheldon, Lionel (Governor), 156–157
Shield, David, 103
Shield, Elizabeth, 103
Shootings. *see also* feuds, posse; Lincoln County War; The Five Day Battle
  of farmhand by Copeland, 21
  of Martin, 25
  of Haskins, 30
  of Patrón, 35–36
  of Casey, 37
  and the law, 45–56
  of Tunstall, 78
  of McCloskey, 81
  of McSween, 98
  of Chapman, 107–109
  of Patrón, 145–150
  of Bonney, 165
Sisneros, Manuel Antonio, 135
Sisters of Charity, 64
Sisters of Loretto, 5–6, 64
Smith, Sam, 120
South, Wilson L., 70
St. Francis Catholic Church, 58
St. Michael's College, 8–11, 162
St. Miguel's Church, 8
St. Nicholas Hotel murder, 136–137
Steck, Michael (Dr.), 141–142
Stock Grower, 153

T

Tafoya, Sambrano (Padre), 126
tax problems and fund misappropriations, 33–35
tax problems and posse feuds, 91–92
"Texas Jack", 118
"The House". *see* Murphy and Co.
Tiedemann, H. G. (Dr.), 22
Tipton, Maria Dolores Felipa Patrón, 144, 161
Tomasine, Pascuali, 65
torreon, 32, 48, 94
tower, Lincoln. *see torreon*
town meeting document, 89–90
train. *see* railroad
Trujillo, Franco, 154–155
Trujillo, Seferino, 25
Tularos Ditch War, 23
Tunstall, John Henry
  meets McSween, 39–40
  travels with Patrón, 41–44
  photo of, *41f*
  on Lincoln, 45–46
  description of, 47
  forms alliance with McSween, 48–52
  and jailbreak, 55
  and the Lincoln County War, 74–87
Tunstall Store, 49
Turner, Marion (Deputy), 97, 112, 123

W

Waite, Fred, 76–78, 83, 87, 112
Waldo, Henry, 121
Wallace, Lew (Governor)
  at first train celebration, 62
  as new governer, 102–103
  photo of, *103f*
  and Chapman letters, 106–110
  arrest list, 112–113
  and Bonney testimony, 113–114
  and Lincoln County Rifles, 114–115
  and Bonney testimony, 116
  and Lincoln County Rifles, 117–119
  appeal to President Hayes, 119
  and Lincoln County Rifles, 123–124
  writes *Ben Hur: A Tale of the Christ*, 164
Wallace's arrest list, 112–113
Walz, Edgar, 107
Warner, Dave, 24–25
wedding customs, 27
wedding massacre, 26–28

CPSIA information can be obtained at www.ICGtesting.com
Printed in the USA
BVOW070445070313

314938BV00002B/57/P